This Book Belongs To

dpInk

Donnalnk Publications, L.L.C.

Moondust Media

STOLEN LULLABIES
Secret Impasses

*Donna*Ink Publications, L.L.C.

dpInk
Donnaink Publications, L.L.C.

U.S.A.

STOLEN & LULLABIES

Secret Impasses

DONNA L.
QUESINBERRY

dpInk
Donnalnk Publications, L.L.C.

DonnaInk Publications, L.L.C.
17611 Aquasco Road, Annapolis, MD 20613
Visit our website(s) at www.donnaink.shop | www.donnalquesinberry.com

This book is a work of literature - poetry. Names, characters, places, and incidents are nonfiction with creative guise. Some actual events, locales, persons, living or dead, are included; however, narrative takes literary privilege. Poems are creative works. Backstories are original nonfiction narrative coupled with artistic expression. Reviews are nonfiction. Content is the sole expression and opinion of the author and not that of the Publisher. No warranties or guarantees are expressed or implied.

First Paperback: March 2015. First Electronic: August 2015. First Hardcover: July 2025.

Library of Congress Cataloging in Publication Data

Ms. Donna L. Quesinberry, 2025 -
    Stolen Lullabies & Secret Impasses / Quesinberry, Donna L. – 2nd Ed.
                      ISBN: 978-1-960431-41-7 (hardback aka)
    296 p.cm.

Summary: "*Stolen Lullabies & Secret Impasses* is a lyrical collection by Donna L. Quesinberry that explores the quiet power of resilience, feminine mysticism, and poetic healing. Each verse unveils stories once silenced, transforming sorrow into spiritual grace and emotional revelation. It's poetry for those ready to reclaim their voice—and rise." ~ Foreword from Ms. Sage Sweetwater – Poet, Screenwriter, Filmmaker.

[BIO005000 BIOGRAPHY & AUTOBIOGRAPHY / Entertainment & Performing Arts, BIO026000 BIOGRAPHY & AUTOBIOGRAPHY / Memoirs, BIO009000 BIOGRAPHY & AUTOBIOGRAPHY / Philosophers, BIO032000 BIOGRAPHY & AUTOBIOGRAPHY / Social Activists, BIO038000 BIOGRAPHY & AUTOBIOGRAPHY / Survival, BIO022000 BIOGRAPHY & AUTOBIOGRAPHY / Women, OCC032000 BODY, MIND & SPIRIT / Angels & Spirit Guides, OCC019000 BODY, MIND & SPIRIT / Inspiration & Personal Growth, OCC010000 BODY, MIND & SPIRIT / Mindfulness & Meditation, OCC014000 BODY, MIND & SPIRIT / New Thought, OCC020000 BODY, MIND & SPIRIT / Prophecy, POE005010 POETRY / American / General, POE023080 POETRY / Subjects & Themes / Motivational & Inspirational, POE024000 POETRY / Women Authors, FAM001010 FAMILY & RELATIONSHIPS / Abuse / Child Abuse, FAM001030 FAMILY & RELATIONSHIPS / Abuse / Domestic Partner Abuse, SEL001000 SELF-HELP / Abuse]

I. Title. II. Title: Stolen Lullabies & Secret Impasses
Dewey Classification: 811.6

10   9   8   7   6   5   4   3   2

2013936118 original edition; 2025XXXXXX 2025 edition.
Printed in the United States of America.

Contents

Foreword by Sage Sweetwater

Women have to say "yes" to this book. Any woman. Every woman. There's a right action, a discourse for every wrong. The content between the covers of "Stolen Lullabies & Secret Impasses" is one of those right actions, coming later in life; sustaining mental health and maintaining dignity arising from child abuse, sexual assault, and domestic violence through the perfected and written word. This valuable work is highly creative and beautifully written, for such a vile topic. This is the ultimate domino theory in reverse, setting them back up after having toppled in the worst of circumstances in the dirty little game of life called family secrets.

A genealogy of a different path on the family tree absolutely branching with unpleasant truths, deeply honest, consistently shocking, revolting, and painfully revealing, assuaged in a beautiful transcript of the author's personal "memoir" written with orderly thought and rationality. This writing is a celebration of healing a multitude of sexual abuses commencing at childhood, present all throughout adulthood.

Gynocentric in literary tour de force, "Stolen Lullabies & Secret Impasses" is a flower in blossom of all that is sacred to a woman's interior, genitalia purged of the weeds in the Sacred Garden of Life. This book is a lifeline to all women; those women who are in the process of healing from sexual abuse in all forms, on the path of retrieval, and those who are healed, embracing an ongoing personal maintenance process. The author, Donna L. Quesinberry has expressed a societal faux pas in such a creative way, through spirituality, through poetry, fact, and personal narrative. The author is intellectually at the right place, and present in mind during the writing, which is cathartic and wise. She has given her readers a palpable understanding of what happens to women forever changes who and what we are. This volume belongs on the bookstore and library shelves in the sections under "Women's Psychology" and (accommodating the fad of creating sections by major chain booksellers) "Painful Lives."

ELDER ABUSE

A SILENT EPIDEMIC

over
5.9 Million
reported cases of elder abuse in 2010

1 in 9 Americans
over 60 has
experienced abuse

only
1 in 23

cases of elder abuse in the U.S. is reported

Preface

Ms. Donna L. Quesinberry (Q) began writing stark performance poetry prior to having a formal knowledge of the term "minimalist," which shares extremely compressed poems such as those compiled in the twenties by the Dadaists[1]. Perhaps, in a previous lifetime, Q was herself a Dadaist, certainly she is one today.

Bob Grumman in *MNMLST POETRY: Un-acclaimed but Flourishing*, shared:

> . . . . *Minimalist poetry was made by the concrete poetry movement of the 50's and 60's before it succumbed to narrowness of scope and various forms of parochialism. The flowering of the haiku in the West was a large influence, as well. To my mind, though, full-scale minimalist poetry didn't begin in this country and Canada until the one-word poems of Aram Saroyan and Richard Kostelanetz in the late sixties and early seventies. The movement, if it can be called that, was almost invisible until the mid-eighties when poets like Geof Huth, Jonathan Brannen, Karl Kempton and others joined it.*

Stolen Lullabies & Secret Impasses is a collection of works from the 1990's through 2010 that relate to the human psyche, familial and interpersonal relationships. As well, it touches on sociology and famiology[2] that results in child abuse, sexual assault, and domestic violence. There are no significant chapter markers in this title and there is no capitalization throughout most of

---

[1]   The style and techniques of a group of artists, writers, etc., of the early 20th century who explored accidental and incongruous effects in their work and who programmatically challenged established canons of art thought, morality, etc.

[2]   A word coined by "Q" for Stolen Lullabies and Secret Impasses.

the works. For this compilation, one word carries no greater or lesser weight than its successor or predecessor.

A back story follows each poem. Approximately one-half of the works share release date reviews from digital forums, print magazines, publications and/or poet and reader websites. Unfortunately, reviews for all poetry were not previously captured and are not available for this edition. Ms. Quesinberry desired to have all reviewers noted for all the referenced work but could not achieve this goal in time for publication. The release of this book has been delayed frequently and Q wanted to complete it in time for 2015's awareness season.

However, all existing reviews are featured after back stories, where they remained available – some are lost to time. It is the hope of the Publisher, and Ms. Quesinberry, readers reflect on the reviews in addition to the poems and back stories as they often feature as much, and at times more, creative license as Q's poems themselves.

Acknowledgement

To my family, friends, and others who created emotive moments in my life . . . I want to thank each of you for your music, which resulted in this poetry. Like synapses are to concepts, the important people in life have been marrow to words for me. And, as Mr. Wayne Dyer says upon rising each day . . *thank you, thank you, thank you, and thank you.*

Additional kudos to everyone from *Aesop's, Authors Den, Blackmail Press, Journal of the Minds, Performance Poetry, Poetry Repairs, Spoken Word* and a myriad of other late 1990's to mid-2000's poetry websites. Al the gifted thinkers who cultivated cross-sections of minimalist, performance and spoken word poetry . . . I have been blessed to spend time in your encampments. Criticisms, mentoring and validations aided all of us collectively in the achievement of evolutionary art forms using written and spoken words . . . such genius. I hope this compilation does justice to our time shared in these artistic hives of the past.

Critics and reviewers carry a special place in my heart because their advice, consideration and time really bolsters writs. Admirations, and cogitation of works, epitomize the world we amassed while serving as muse and a continuous driver to achieve more. Therefore, it seems appropriate to include saved reviews after each poem's back story.

And a special thanks to the English teacher from Surrattsville High School in Clinton Maryland who made language exciting and fun and refreshing. Unfortunately, I cannot remember her name but I recall how much more I loved English when she taught as well as every year thereafter. Thank you for making literature real for me in a way no one had accomplished previous to my experiences in your classroom, I'll do my research to include you appropriately in future works.

"LOOK AT IT THIS WAY.
AT LEAST YOU WEREN'T A VIRGIN."
Most people don't know what to say. *We do.*
SEXUAL ASSAULT
resource line
(800) 825-7273

Introduction

Words are an act of exhumation. When they fuse well the result is a synaptic rhythm coupled with expressive vitality. In *Stolen Lullabies & Secret Impasses*, intimate works predominantly the collection. Cathartic in nature, these works remove wall-upon-wall of clutter, which otherwise hampers a free-flow of consciousness. The all-encompassing nature of topics contained in each of these poems are evidentiary of the strong effort to liberate my conscious at the time(s) when compositions were conceived.

Poetry and prose also ignite humanity's essence in an artful manner while propelling it heavenward to reveal all things sacrosanct. Works cited in *Stolen Lullabies & Secret Impasses* expose shavings of residual angst derived from child abuse, sexual assault, and domestic violence. These loiterers linger amid post-traumatic stress (PTSD) niggles that promise ongoing adverse residual effects in spite of positive outcomes. Violence becomes part of the whole self.

Having sustained an egregious sexual assault as a twelve (12) year old child, the veracities of abuse, assault, and violence remain ever-present in my life-time of wordplay. This is not; however, by intent.

Acts of savagery are more than short-lived corporal and psychological wrongs. Rather, they are longstanding behemoths rearing their ugly heads time and time and time again throughout a survivor's existence no matter the level of recovery. Life after the fact results in ongoing skirmishes with inner demons throughout a victim's lifetime. Most of the poetry in this compilation is relative to those wounds, which are excised by the scalpel of the written word.

Additionally, a few of the dirges presented reveal irreverent escapism. Some are dream quests. Lastly, a few focus on love but mostly anatomize love's dictums. Again, all prose in *Stolen Lullabies & Secret Impasses* is seasoned with an obscurity abuse, assault and violence convey in underlying sentient truths.

Readers from all walks of life are appreciated here. It is my genuine hope, practical awareness regarding the short- and long-term effects of abuse, assault, and violence stem from reading, *Stolen Lullabies & Secret Impasses*.

Thank you.

Dedication

To the all, the five, the two, the multitude, the one — keep the cage doors open and think of me when I am gone.

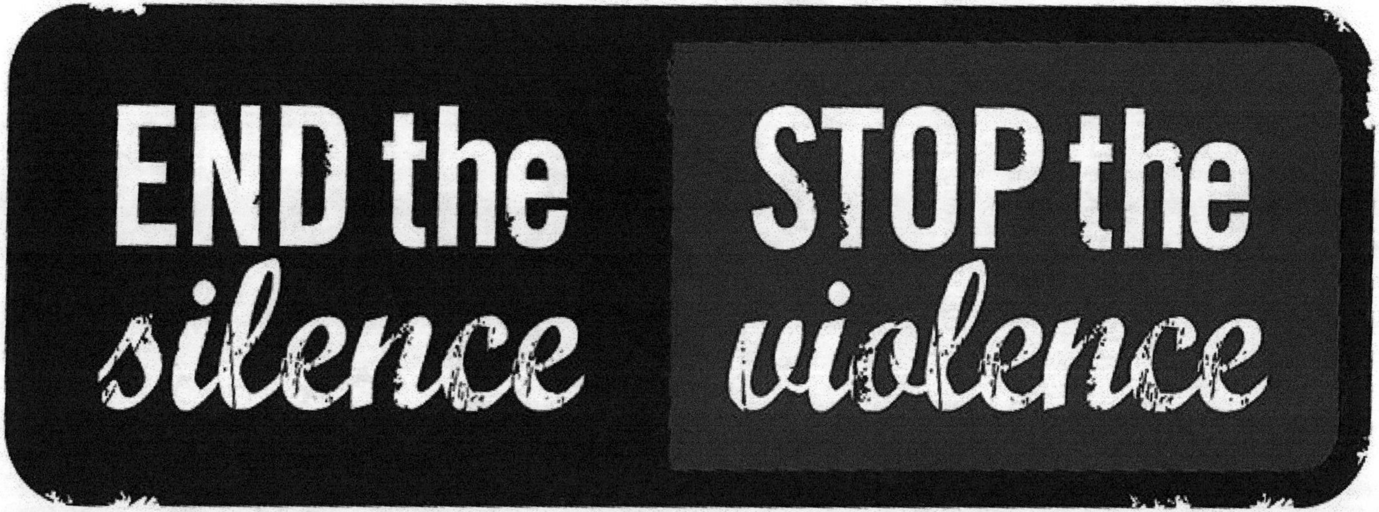
END the silence
STOP the violence

STOLEN LULLABIES
Secret Impasses

Blue Ribbons
for Kids

Help Keep Kids Safe
& Families Strong

Prologue

Stolen Lullabies & Secret Impasses reflects on wrongful acts, which play a pivotal role as muse for this collection of poetry. The Extro contained at title close presents Presidential Proclamations, Awareness Campaigns and their materials, and informative literature links concerning:

Child Abuse and Neglect	Sexual Assault	Domestic Violence

As a daughter, sister, wife, mother and individual, I've unfortunately been exposed to each of these unnatural predilections of the human condition. Raised in a good home, with loving parents, who had the best of intentions to rear successful children, with no undue burdens in an upper middle-class lifestyle . . . malice still found its path and darkened the doorway of my life. The sad truth is child abuse, sexual assault, and domestic violence affect all walks of life regardless of station.

Though a stalwart survivor and recoveree, haunting aftereffects persist. No matter the level of discernment or assuagement, certain aspects of life and relationships remain eternally challenged post-violence; relationships are tainted at the very least due to the wrongs of toxic acts. Basic tenets of faith, trust and comfort . . . essential to qualitative interactions among family, friends, associates or lovers are tenuous at best for all survivors of mental and/or physical cruelty.

And, then there's the little things . . . such as . . .

Never being able to rough house and have my head covered because if my head gets covered, a primal creature materializes - fists engaged in fight or flight fashion. This is not uncommon for recoverees. For most of us, there are idiosyncrasies no one else would comprehend "if" we cared to share them. We have become greatly attuned to diminutive innuendos otherwise overlooked by workmates, associates and acquaintances – we've "seen" danger up close and personal. We recognize it.

Violence is prevalent around the planet, so some people no longer direct their attention toward it. After all, it is unpleasant. There is a tendency to over-look the indications of abuse and neglect, assault and violence. Tendencies of wrongdoers are often demonstrated in an ambiguous manner. We get a sense of danger, we suspect something but often don't listen to our intuition, which is correct more often than not.

Survivors conceal minefields of personal revelations resulting from the travesties bad experiences leave behind. Unfortunately, apprehensions concern-ing "impending peril," having bedded it in the past, are seemingly innocuous to everyone else because the level of awareness for survivors is heightened. Very often, folks involved with former victims believe they are over sensitized.

So . . . the replevied learn to hide their *Secret Impasses.*

Post-assault coping mechanisms tend to strain social and familial engage-ments. No matter how wonderful or good a human bond . . . past abuse, assault, and violence is never an erstwhile act. Positive outcomes remain arduous at best and due to this reality; greater mindfulness is required in the here and now.

The prevention of child abuse, sexual assault, and domestic violence is where focus should today and beyond.

Works in *Stolen Lullabies & Secret Impasses* share glimpses of the con-ceptual impediments trauma leaves in its wake. It is my sincere intent for these works to enlighten, educate, and, of course, entertain. My objective remains to ease others' suffering through the pretense of indulgence while sharing certain knowledge: "As survivors, we are not alone."

In the Extro, at the close of this title, as previously stated, are United States Presidential Proclamations, Awareness Campaigns and associated information for reader participation in awareness and prevention. The *Voices Beyond the Impasse: The Reclamation Movement* was released April of 2016 and I was happy to join in radio or other programming to speak out and affirm the awareness campaigns created by others.

Regarding sales and contributions: each title sold is included in a graduated charitable donation plan. Initially, 10K copies sold delivers 10% roya ty donation in equal shares to awareness campaigns. As sales increase, percentages of royalty donations are raised by 5% for every 10K copies sold until 100K copies are delivering 60% of royalties as charitable gifts. Once 100K titles plus are sold, 70% of royalties are to be distributed among awareness campaigns.

love.life.memories.................................

The back stories for each poem share personal narrative and revelations, which have not been shared throughout my lifetime for the most part. Within these back stories, the "love.life.memories" divider separates the general narrative from the "about the poem" narrative.

Due to being raped at a very young age, disclosure remained taboo concerning sexual assault; post-secondary child abuse and domestc violence, which is often the result of early life traumas of this nature. Because the attack I suffered was brutal in nature, it was never mentioned in our home after the initial shock and horror. It was determined best to be forgotten. For a restorative measure, and out of my parents' kindness, I was provided horses, horse trailers, equestrian supplies, and horsewomanship training as well as transport to competitions. Naturally, I moved on toward becoming an avid equestrian.

For years, life transpired as if I were never sexually assaulted at all, and to this day, Mother cannot discuss the trauma I sustained and becomes upset if it is mentioned. So much time has passed, it isn't much of a cons deration to force the subject in the current hour – we have all grown much older. But sexual acts of violence do result in mental anguish and ill-effects such as marrying abusers believing a personal history of assault is a culmination of terms of endearment. I know this firsthand because it did for me and it did for my five children until I learned to stand-up to an abusive husband, to say "no" and to leave and manage as a single mother on my own. It also did for my extended family, siblings and neighborhood friends too. Suffice it to say, relationships become scathed because not speaking out about the crime of abuse, assault and violence means a lot is being said in silence.

This is perhaps one of the worst things about violence . . . it has a past. In developing awareness, a deliberate universal recalibration regarding "how we reflect" on family secrets such as these, or historical archives, needs to create a dynamic shift in our thinking. We need *To Stop Allowing Lullabies To Be Stolen And See The Secret Impasses For What They Are*[3].

Airing out generational closets, no matter who they belong to, how painful or unpleasant, opens dialogue for recovery. In order to heal ~ it is something each of us should do ~ because statistics state every reader of this book, and any other book, is exposed to child abuse, sexual assault and/or domestic violence because someone in their inner circle, or they themselves, have been victimized. Healing is where our hearts, minds and energies should be focused.

For me, releasing this title is a first step in the culmination of personal reclamation. I've done the work in my past without disclosure, except through minimalist poetry among select audiences. There is no reason to hide from the veracity of reconciliation ~ I'm allowing the twelve (12) year old in me to shed her dirty secrets without fear, blame or reprisal ~ it is time to open her cage door and set her free. And, for the woman who sustained beatings at the hands of her husband, who was supposed to have and to hold, to love and protect, in sickness and in health . . . finally – the ability to stand firm and state, "I don't accept your violence anymore."

I want to thank each of you for taking time from the business of living, and activities of life, to read, *Stolen Lullabies & Secret Impasses*. And I want to tell my family – my five children, my mother, my sister and brother and their families . . . I love you. And, to my daddy, grandparents and loved ones in heaven – thank you for the profound strengths of our shared lineage. When we have suffered, we have all done so together.

Thankfully, the brilliance of life, survival, forgiveness, and joy have out-weighed the clouds of evil. Our many wonderful life events, I intend to share in upcoming releases but I do want readers to know with this title . . . the blessings of my family and our overall strengths moved me toward enlightenment through an ancestral innate ability to overcome and conquer malice within our generation.

---

[3]   *Stop Allowing Lullabies to be Stolen and See the Secret Impasses for What They Are!* is Ms. Donna L. Quesinberry's Awareness Campaign beginning April 2015 for child abuse, sexual assault and domestic violence – check out the "join the mailing list" chapter and/or write to special_markets@donnaink.com to learn more.

Epigraph

"Offer them what they secretly want and they of course immediately become panic-stricken."

~ Jack Kerouac

EVERYONE HAS A ROLE
TO PLAY IN PROTECTING
CHILDREN

don's Faire

twine and cord
        grappled with it all day
        walked the dog
        remembered-
        mothers reproach
        an echo
        permanently captured porch
        then ledge.

steaks thawed. dual dining
        with singular exclamation,
        no appetite will
        go undone-
        he's unleashed.
        focused on Sony PlayStation
        moment of the gift.
        Mary's acid played

an oasis tune on repeat
        twenty dollars
        hard and worked savings to
        count on. Mary, mother.
        calls-rings-busy.

she leaves a message
someone else's line handles the blame.
pledge-dusting done.

plaque reads: good son
      grandma rests next door.
      grass blows sweet
      anchored with salty water
      oak leans close.
      Sony people linger
      view new neighbors
      readings - names, dates, histories

      warning them to go easy
            bringing clouds down
                  sending their son home.

Jon's Faire Back Story

Our sweet, and dear, unofficially adopted brother and son Jon, took his own life after cleaning the house and walking his family's dog. He set the dinner table,

Published in New Zealand's B l a c k m
a i l P r e s s 3, ISSN 1176-4791 in
March of 2002 – Guest Editor
Christina Conrad

thawed steaks, and put an Oasis song on repeat on his Sony PlayStation my children had gifted to him. At approximately noon, he determined to call his mother. He was in tears and needed to talk. After their conversation, his mom asked his step-sister to call him and talk with him as she worked to get someone in their family to go home to visit with him until she could get there. No one was available until later in the afternoon and then it was too late. And his mother's actions are not unlike many mothers who juggle work and parenting . . . she did her best.

Despondent, Jon took the dog's leash and hung himself over the balcony. He was found by a neighbor at the end of their workday. He had been at our home just the evening prior and was in good spirits. He intended to visit the next day after school – as usual – but he stayed home from school the following day after an argument with his mom the night before. During their argument, she later told me she had suggested to him we probably hated to see him at our home every day.

I answered her, "We love Jon. We love his visits."

Having just had the pleasure of his presence the evening prior, and every day after school of every week that school year, our family was in extreme shock to hear of his suicide. We could not believe it. We didn't even realize he was depressed. He never appeared depressed at our home. And, to this day, each of us wonders, *Why did Jon take his life?*

Suicide is malignancy. Those who have to deal with it question what could have been done differently or if anything was done differently would have mattered. It is a never-ending story of considerations and, "What ifs." Doctors suggest someone, anyone, intent on suicide are going to do what they intend regardless of our interaction with them. Some psychologists told me we may have prolonged Jon's life by being there for him and that we shouldn't feel it was our fault. But that doesn't help.

One of my daughters had a crush on Jon and she remains curious if she'd shared this with him, would it have been the catalyst for him to determine to stay alive? We often love people in our lives and fear sharing our feelings . . . but would our feelings voiced help those we love? Of course, we all know of unrequited love, and sharing our feelings in those instances often results in despondency, so it is a two-edged sword to be open regarding our private feelings . . . as the cliché goes.

One of my sons, Jon clung too. My son often felt overwhelmed by the clinginess. He later thought, "What if I'd been more open to friend shipping and had not gotten aggravated about having a friend who always wanted to hang out with me? Would he be alive now?" Even though my son was a good friend, he believes he could have been a better friend. Oftentimes, we could all be better friends — maybe we should. However, with mental health concerns and suicide, we can't really blame ourselves for not having done more because we may be doing more than average already. Suicidal tendencies involve a person's internal hardwiring more often than not and no matter what our level of involvement, we are not equipped to deal with those matters.

Albeit, as a single mother of five children, having heard me many a time, over many a year say . . . "I'm going to take a long jump off a short pier," along with other insidious generational remarks shared over the eons with no "actual" ill intent. Those commentaries, passed down from mother to daughter through the generations, without active thought, emitted in sarcasm are wielded much like the slip of a swear word when the mind is preoccupied. But what if comments have an impact on individuals who are external to our familial annals of wrongful commentaries to alleviate stress? In my family's history, those passing remarks remain mental cast-offs for ventilation of grey matter after an arduous day, week, month or year. In that guise, they remain understood as nothing more than verbal fodder. But to our guests — are our conversational cast-offs taken at face value?

I reflect on things said in the day-to-day now and wonder if I should not have uttered such negativity within earshot of our young guest. While not real preoccupations or real considerations and often said in jest . . . today I hurt in reflecting on the many times I uttered, "If I were gone tomorrow, they'd surely feel bad for not hearing and seeing me today." What selfish commentary, and I do pray for forgiveness even now . . . mostly for the ability to forgive myself. Certainly, I heard that sentence all the years of my life from my mother and her from hers.

I wonder too, did following my mother's advice to reduce the number of child guests to our home, in order to reduce stressors, I was under as a single parent of five children, create an ever so slight emotional withdrawal this young man who I thought of as a son, felt, sensed and reacted to? Did my actions cause greater anguish for him and result in our loss? Certainly, my mother's suggestions were to help me and well-advised. I didn't reduce Jon's visits and told him he was always welcome as I felt he was one of my children for all intents and purposes at that time but I'll never know the answer to that question because he committed suicide. We can no longer share conversation and he is eternally missed.

I often speculate, do none of these things matter? Are we all perhaps just a little too self-imported believing our actions actually affect the decision-making of a potential suicide victim? Why can't we believe his decision of dying was his own? Better yet, were there signs we should have noticed and responded to?

As a footnote, one of my daughter's best friends had a dream about Jon two weeks prior to his suicide. It was a vivid dream and depicted him hung from the porch; however, in her dream someone accidentally killed him and staged a hanging. After the initial trauma of his death . . . we realized the dream, she'd shared two weeks earlier unfolded. To this day, we also wonder concerning her dream and whether or not it was an otherworldly message we should have tapped into.

Love.Life.memories.............................

The blow of a loss of a gentile spirit who always greets others with smiles and positive commentary is life-altering. After the passing of such a giant consciousness, a true golden child, who we all had the honor to grow to love as an unofficial surrogate brother and son - "jon's faire" came to fruition.

As my children would, I'd much rather see Jon outside of the realm of the written word. It would be such a joy to hear him ask to taste test yet another pot of edibles on our kitchen stove after school, and to hear him call me "Mom" no matter how make believe it was for us both. It would be heavenly to hear Jon's voice and see his smile today.

We pray you rest easy, sweet Jon - you are eternally loved and remembered.

IN 1829, A 20-YEAR-OLD

ABRAHAM LINCOLN

LOST CONTROL AND NEARLY

KILLED HIMSELF.

HE TRIED TO END HIS AGONY

WITH A GUN,

BUT FRIENDS STOPPED HIM.

SUICIDE PREVENTION LIFELINE.ORG
WHOSE LIFE WILL YOU SAVE?

Salvation's Angels

viewing — predominance
　　　　unscathed.
　　　　they peer
　　　　effortlessly.

beguiling – dominions
        untouched.
        they design
        relentlessly.

quieting - natter
        unloved.
        they reason
        naturelessly.

forsaking— sentinels
        unknown.
        they fly
        middenlessly.

remaining — muted
        lest
        they understand
        indolentlessly.

Salvation's Angels Back Story

Before angels and related folklore became Art Nouveau, I ceveloped a preoccupation. As a survivor, the otherworldly realm is where I often rested my head much of the time. I found; supranormal events not only existed but they were sanctioned practices. Many years later, I was evaluated and diagnosed as precognitive with strong extra sensory perception (ESP) skills. I concluded I was naturally drawn to angels and spiritualism coupled with a faith in God because these were safe connections. At least, safer than human contact had proven for me.

At age sixteen, I was engaged to marry a young man my parents liked who I had a strong case of puppy love for. He and I shared mutual pass on as teen-agers. Being very young when he asked me to marry him, I was determined to graduate high school a year early with full honors. Afterward, my parents provided their letter of consent (conveying my hand in marriage and meeting state legal requirements) to marry. Our big wedding (nearly one hundred and fifty people) ensued after our one-year engagement.

I went from age sixteen (16) to my wedding day and vows, having just turned seventeen (17) a few weeks prior. I was indeed a young bride. My husband and I embarked on what we'd believed to be our journey, after the wedding reception. Mike was Pentecostal and believed in the supernatural phenomenon of speaking in tongues, as it was commensurate with religion. There was a lot of talk of avoiding the devil and his evil designs towards Christians in the Pentecostal Church. This was often accompanied by true-to-life occurrences. Seeing dishes fly off shelves and "other" phantom events, pretty much solidified to me, *something was attacking Christians and we needed intervention.*

Miracles were commonplace as well. Healing of broken limbs and other inspiring acts, I personally witnessed. Having done so, I grew to understand and accept there is, at the minimum, a strong relationship between enhanced belief and supranormal phenomenon, such as telekinesis. To this day, the phenomena I witnessed remain in my mind as . . . miracles because they defy logic.

Noting apparitions and telekinetic activities, it wasn't long before extended family members spoke in tongues too, which was never well-received by the men. Father wasn't pleased by it all. However, it is said today, "Speaking in tongues was once viewed as an occurrence exclusive to Pentecostal believers but it now transcends traditional denominational boundaries to include Baptists, Episcopalians, Lutherans, Methodists, Presbyterians, and Roman Catholics. The condition of a person when in this state has been described as ecstasy, frenzy, trance, and/or hypnotic. Some call it a hysterical experience. There is a mystique and charisma associated with speaking in tongues or glossolalia[4].

"Contrary to what may be a common perception, studies suggest people who speak in tongues rarely suffer from mental problems. A recent study of nearly 1,000 evangelical Christians in England found those who engaged in the practice were more emotionally stable than those who did not. Researchers have identified at least two forms of practice, one ecstatic and frenzied, the other subdued and nearly silent. These findings contrasted sharply with images taken of other spiritually inspired mental states like meditation, which is often a highly focused mental exercise, activating the frontal lobes.

"'Scans showed a dip in the activity of a region called the left caudate. The findings from the frontal lobes are very clear, and make sense, but the caudate is usually active when you have positive affects, pleasure, positive emotions,' said Dr. James A. Coan, a psychologist at the University of Virginia.

"'So, it's not so clear what that finding says about speaking in tongues. The caudate area is also involved in motor and emotional control,' Dr. Newberg said, 'so it may be that practitioners, while mindful of their circumstances, nonetheless cede some control over their bodies and emotions.'" [5]

According to the University of Virginia and The New York Times, what was once considered frenzied overstimulation during our seemingly blessed, and simultaneously cursed marriage, due to the ascriptions of speaking in tongues . . . would be quid pro quo today. There is some personal resolution in that knowledge for me.

---

4   A form of glossolalia in which a person experiencing religious ecstasy utters incomprehensible sounds believed to be of divine inspiration. Also called gift of tongues.
5   Carey, Benedict (2006). *A Neuroscientific Look at Speaking in Tongues*. The New York Times – Health Section.

When I became pregnant with my eldest son, after our brief six (6) months of marriage, I believed I had the flu due to my level of naiveté. My teenaged husband was overjoyed and overwhelmed simultaneously; however, he was truly leaning toward joy initially. He rushed out right off the bat and bought a HUGE teddy bear for our impending baby at only six (6) weeks conception. And it was life-size . . . so cute.

Shortly thereafter, his family began intimidating him concerning the depth of responsibility a child brings and he began to change. He suddenly believed we were living in a vision much like the movie, "Devil's Advocate" where the central character experiences a life-time of catastrophic events wh le washing his hands in a courthouse bathroom where he was an attorney. In what appeared to be mere seconds, a life-time traversed in the lead character's lucid dream. During the transportation, he made decisions, which resulted in his reawakening at the courthouse sink overwhelmed by what seemed to have actually transpired involving an evil plot of the Devil to claim the world. My husband believed we were, like the movie, living in a dream state. He believed it was a test for us to see the true to life battle of Heaven verses Hell. To this day, I believe he still believes he's in the vision.

Of course, he suffered a nervous breakdown. And, in coping with it and him, I learned any argument I was poised to suggest we were not in a dream – tested the veracity of his faith and therefore his sanity. It was a dangerous scenario. If I said, "Let's call someone and go visit," he ascribed me to a weakened state and would suggest I was listening to the Devil in my disbelief. It goes without saying, mitigating the situation was delicate. The result was the dissolution of our marriage once it was all over with.

There was mayhem, and hardship, during this crisis of faith to him; and a realization I needed to escape the religion by me. He had neurotic parents (according to psychologists who were thankfully Indian ascribing his incident to a deep meditation). His parents were extremely over-bearing and they could be cruel, which is a form of abuse. Their actions served as a precursor to an emotional break as they continuously expressed . . . "If only you d not married" . . . "If only you would have joined the Air Force" . . . "If only you weren't strapped with a child" . . . and etc. They pummeled him with negativity and argument. If they had celebrated the impending baby and our marriage – things may have turned a different corner for us but they didn't do so.

About that time, the fact I wasn't a Pentecostal after all, became resolute for me. The religion had felt dangerous for a while because it penned so great a necessity to share fanatical beliefs and paranormal activities occurred far too often. It remains in my mind a pseudoscience at best, where if one follows too intently, it might result in psychosis and/or schizophrenia.

However, being a believer in expanded consciousness and the dimensional underpinnings of life Albert Einstein ascribed to, as well as having a faith in God, I continued to research religious texts in attempt to make sense of what I'd witnessed among the Pentecostal communities.

One of my best friends in high school had traveled extensively around the world with her family. Previous to my first marriage, she had writs such as Kahlil Gibran and Gnostics writings. She was Agnostic, which I did not understand having been raised Southern Baptist but I appreciated her for being broad-minded and intellectual. The works she shared with me prior to my first marriage I often returned to.

As far as angels and all things supranormal, Catholicism presented the most significant declarations regarding them, including the nine realms. The Torah and Koran too, had strong affinities towards angels. So much so, it was hard to understand their cultural dissociative relationship to one another, as their systems of belief parallel in many ways. Over time more and more studies finally culminated in the *Pseudepigrapha, Apocrypha* and *Sacred Writings*, which came to bare when my eldest son prepared to serve a mission and our elders introduced the texts.

In between early studies and Pseudepigrapha, were many books about personal experiences relative to angelic intervention and psychic phenomenon, such as "Where Angels Walk," by Joan Wester Anderson or "Divine Guidance: How to Have a Dialogue with God and Your Guardian Angels," by Doreen Virtue and "Angel-speake: How to Talk With Your Angels," by Barbara Mark and Trudy Griswold. Many people shared stories of being physically saved during unusual and extreme circumstances by guardian angels and/or mysterious visitors. These books shared information apart from standard historical archives concerning angels and mysticism surrounding miracles. Some required citations and research but often none existed. Instead, they presented their claims as revelations. With my longstanding predisposition to angelic lore, mystics, supra- and paranormal research . . . over the years, I was commonly gifted numerous titles and CDs on birthdays and holidays and developed an extensive library – later lost in storage. I soaked up those materials like a sponge.

With this time-honored combination of scholarly texts and urban literature, many unique characteristics of mysticism that centered on angelic lore sprang into my life. And my own life experiences counter-balanced with a pragmatic center as well as comprehension for life beyond the veil of our unidimensional thinking, helped me during years of growth and introspection.

Love.Life.memories.................................

For "salvation's angels," the years of dabbling in attempts to capture angelic mysticism and the consternation of creatures outside our realm of existence resulted in this poem. While it was never one of my personally favored works; feedback remained curiously positive by readers and critics alike. Due to this, and the nature of its history, I choose to include it in this compilation.

STOP
DOMESTIC VIOLENCE

Get Involved, Safe A Life

My Mummy

breast rises to these lips
thirst stricken and aching
to drink the nectar of being

womb relinquished, resigned her fruits
to tender and supple flesh
poignant is the creative force

lips parting, engage lactation of experience
soft, untainted, cradling all i can be
gracious touch, angelic care, entrusts you

love borne betwixt we two
developing at the areola of our vortex
our expanse of breath and mammalism

recognition of sacrifice
breasts rising to these lips
bliss of succulence in their release.

My Mummy Back Story

In the late 1950's when I was born, children were bottle-fed for the most part within the contiguous United States. In the 1920s, women's breasts were sexualized and criticism was regarded toward breastfeeding. At that time, and afterward, bottle-feeding was considered the *scientific method of motherhood*, and as such, deemed the best method for feeding infant children[6]. This method allowed women freedom from domesticity as well as one of the supposedly more primal practices of recorded history – the engagement of lactation and human attachment to the breast for the purposes of food rather than stimulation.

Among conventional European circles, it was thought breastfeeding resulted in prolonged oral gratification syndrome. Therefore, bottle-feeding was done state-of-the-art. It was devoid of deviancies associated with oral gratification, which was frowned on at the time. By 1958, sixty-three (63) percent of infants consumed formula directly after birth, and only twenty-one (21) percent breastfed throughout the world[7].

During the upswing of scientific motherhood, many mothers were told they suffered from insufficient milk syndrome (IMS)[8]. Commonly, these mothers could have lactated successfully, however. Since the 1920's, the natural physiology of motherhood to nurse babies from their breast, thereby providing required immunities and other true science-based derivatives found in mothers' milk, has become a process of selection much like birth itself. How to feed an infant has evolved into a practitioner choice where convenience, work requirements and/or desires carry the most significant weight in feeding choices for infants.

While there are no definitive studies on breastfeeding creating a more natural bond thereby reducing infanticide, which is on the rise throughout the globe; it is true in the United States, breastfeeding beyond one (1) year of age

---

6   Lozoff, B. (1998) Explanatory mechanisms for poorer development in iron-deficient anemic infants. *Nutrition, Health and Child Development* 566:162-178 Scientific Publication Pan American Health Organization, The World Bank, and Tropical Metabolism Research Unit.

7   Colle, E., Ayoub, E. & Raile, R. (1958) *Hypertonic dehydration (hypernatremia): the role of feedings high in solutes.* Pediatrics 22:5-12.

8   Akre, J. *Infant Feeding. The Physiological Basis.* 1991. WHO Bulletin OMS 1989; Supplement 67:43,52.
      Dick-Read, G. *Childbirth Without Fear. The Principles and Practice of Natural Childbirth.* Harper & Row 1959; pp.236,238.
      Neville, M.C. and Neifert, M.R. *Lactation. Physiology, Nutrition, and Breast-feeding* Plenum Press 1983; p. 303.
      Raphael, D. *The Tender Gift: Breastfeeding.* Prentice-Hall 1973; pp.67, 136, 194.

is considered extended breastfeeding. This is in contrast to WHO recommend-ations. The American Academy of Pediatrics stated in 1997,

> *"Breastfeeding should be continued for at least the first year of life and beyond for as long as mutually desired by mother and child."*

However, in the United States, breastfeeding beyond the first year of life is often considered sexually stimulating and can result in court action. And, when mothers engage in the practice past one and one-half years of life, it has resulted, in America, in removal of the child from the mother's home.

Sociological Maladies & the Breast

Apart from the science of bottle-feeding vs breastfeeding, there are socio-logical implications. Due to these sociological maladies, many mothers who would have otherwise worked at breastfeeding didn't. And, where milk insuffi-ciency seemed at issue during the early stages of lactation, mothers succumb-ed to the notation they didn't have what it takes to breastfeed – this sentiment still prevails today.

1950's Americana and the Breast

From the 1950's onward, IMS served as reasoning to convey bottles to children. This was normally accompanied by doctor and/or nurse suggestion. Due to this, IMS became widely accepted. Questions remain today, concerning IMS and whether or not it is even a "real" syndrome or if it is truly just a psycho-logical convenience alleviating the guilt associated with not breastfeeding.

In Third World countries, bottle-feeding created severe growth failure due to the lack of high-calorie foods. The condition, marasmus,[9] was caused by dilation of cow's milk formulas. Marasmus is a form of severe developmental breakdown closely connected with high-calorie food loss directly associated to bottle-feeding. Additionally, rickets and blindness due to the lack of Vitamins A and D in early cow's milk or condensed milk products affect many Third World and lower income communities who rely on less expensive formula options. Too, without appropriate refrigeration among world communities, formula contamin-ation results in infections, malnutrition and other illnesses; and infant mortality rates . . . even in non-Third World countries.

---

[9]   Wickes IG. A history of infant feeding. *Part I. Primitive peoples: Ancient works: Renaissance writers. Archives of Disease in Childhood.* 1953a; 28:151–158.

1950's Americana recognized successful women as commercialized . . . they were depicted holding martinis, smoking cigarettes, wearing 50's suits with pillbox hats during pregnancy. Usually, these up-and-coming women were depicted in their third trimester. At the time, of course premature delivery, birth defects and/or cancer were not linked to cigarette smoking nor was infant alcohol syndrome (IAS).

After all, until the association of cigarettes to cancer, tobacco served as one of America's most successful resources and alcohol has remained an international symbol for entertainment and fun.

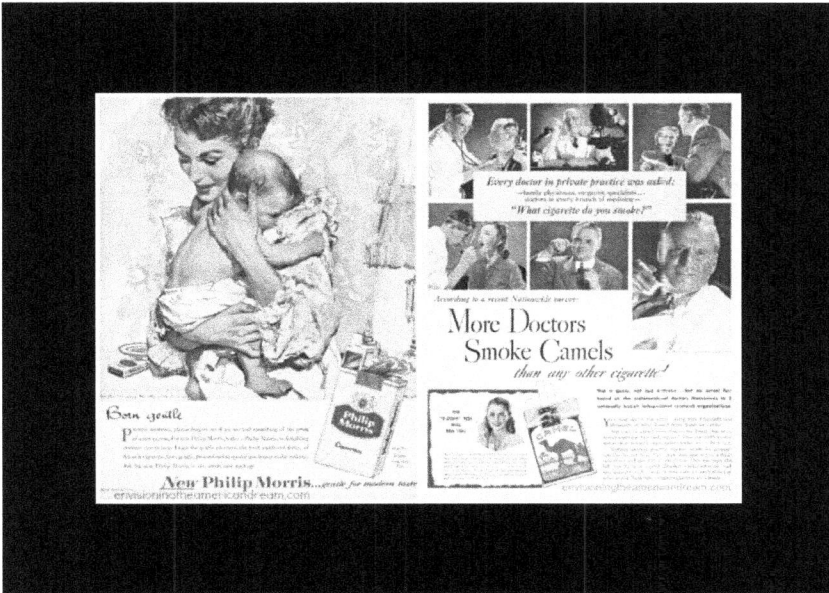

My own mother, being from an upwardly mobile and "good" household, was progressive and accepted the *scientific motherhood methodology* along with the other sixty-three (63) plus percent of her contemporaries[10]. Luckily for us (my siblings and I), she did not smoke nor drink martinis during her lifetime nor pregnancies. However, I remain curious regarding our association as mother and daughter and whether it would have been different had she not been persuaded not to breastfeed.

In yet another era of the breast, and our regard toward infants, during the reinfatuation with all things natural, I birthed five children. Of course, I elected

---

10   Huminick, Sharon. "*The Clinical Significance of Breastmilk Maturation Rates*." Birth 14 (1987):174-79.

to breastfeed, as it was the progressive mindset of the time and a lot of research was provided demonstrating bottle-feeding may not have been such a *scientific motherhood method* after all. At the time, women's breasts fell into two camps, natural or commercial, and women who nursed publicly with a sense of decorum were viewed as naturalist while those who elected not to were considered more professional.

Breastfeeding & Abuse ~ A Correlation?

Some question could be interpreted regarding too, child abuse ratios to breastfeeding ratios. And our over-active association with the breast as a sexual tool contrasted to a mechanism of nature for perpetuation of humanity, might give rise to annals of discourse in the future. Certainly, with sexual assaults and infanticide on the rise – there might be a case for further research to determine if either are the result of our preoccupation with females as devices to fill sexual proclivities and deviancies rather than as mothers, sisters, daughters and equals.

Mothers generally enjoy nursing children. This is largely due to a hormone-like substance called oxytocin[11], which is released as a consequence of nursing and holding their infants. Levels are based on the amount of this contact. Oxytocin produces uterine contractions during labor, is strongly involved in mother-child bonding after birth and during breastfeeding relationship, it is also released during sexual intercourse. Also, blood levels rise in response to touch, warmth, and even when remembering a positive relationship. Oxytocin is released in the brain chiefly in response to social contact but its release is especially pronounced with skin-to-skin contact. This hormone has been called the "love hormone" or the "cuddle hormone" or the "bonding hormone." It provides a sense of calm and wellbeing, promotes bonding patterns and creates desire for further contact with individuals inciting its release. It helps mothers and their children to bond together. It is involved in those mothering feelings experienced after giving birth to a child.

Since it is present during sexual intercourse, it also helps men and women bond in order to form lasting relationships. It makes them want to be close and affectionate toward one another. Without oxytocin, animals don't recognize or remember their partner though they are able to recognize objects. Autistic

---

11   Coiro, V., Alboni, A., Gramellini, D., Cigarini, C., Bianconi, L., Pignatti, D. Volpi, R. & Chiodera, P. (1992). *Inhibition by ethanol of the oxytocin response to breast stimulation in normal women and the role of endogenous opioids*. Acta Endocrinol. 126, 213-216.

children (who often have difficulty with social relationships) have lowered levels of this hormone[12].

Oxytocin is not the only part of the chemical soup produced in our bodies when we cuddle and feel close to our children. Opioids (pleasure hormones) are natural morphine-like chemicals that reduce pain awareness and create feelings of elation. Social contacts, particularly touch - especially between parent and child – induce opioid release, creating good feelings and further enhance bonding – so there might be some validity to breastfeeding as an abuse and neglect deterrent.

The fact that in America, and other "civilized" nations, we ascribe the breast to sexuality and gratification rather than physiology and nurturing seems directly correlative to abuse, assault and violent tendenc es, which are above average. There are no conclusive studies readily available to make a declarative statement regarding this assertion currently, however. But I wonder.

Love.Life.memories...............................

Throughout these sociological and scientific dilemmas associated with feeding my infant children, the bonds of motherhood always appeared to fall to the wayside among many contemporaries. It was during my personal observation of this obvious oversight I penned, "my mummy."

In my reflections on motherhood, mother to child bonding, and infant development I noted Mary, the depiction of all things good in motherhood as the Mother of Jesus Christ – regardless of religious or agnostic designation – remained an illustration of morality in revelation of the human breast. Oftentimes, art demonstrates Mary feeding Jesus with her breast exposed with zero sexualization.

This work is not meant to make an assertion regarding right or wrong of bottle-feeding vs. breastfeeding; it is my personal expose' regarding an infant's acceptance of sustenance and the lifelong recourse that follows the decision to breastfeed or not.

---

12   O. Peñagarikano et al., *"Exogenous and evoked oxytocin restores social behavior in the Cntnap2 mouse model of autism,"* Science Translational Medicine, 7:271ra8, 2015.

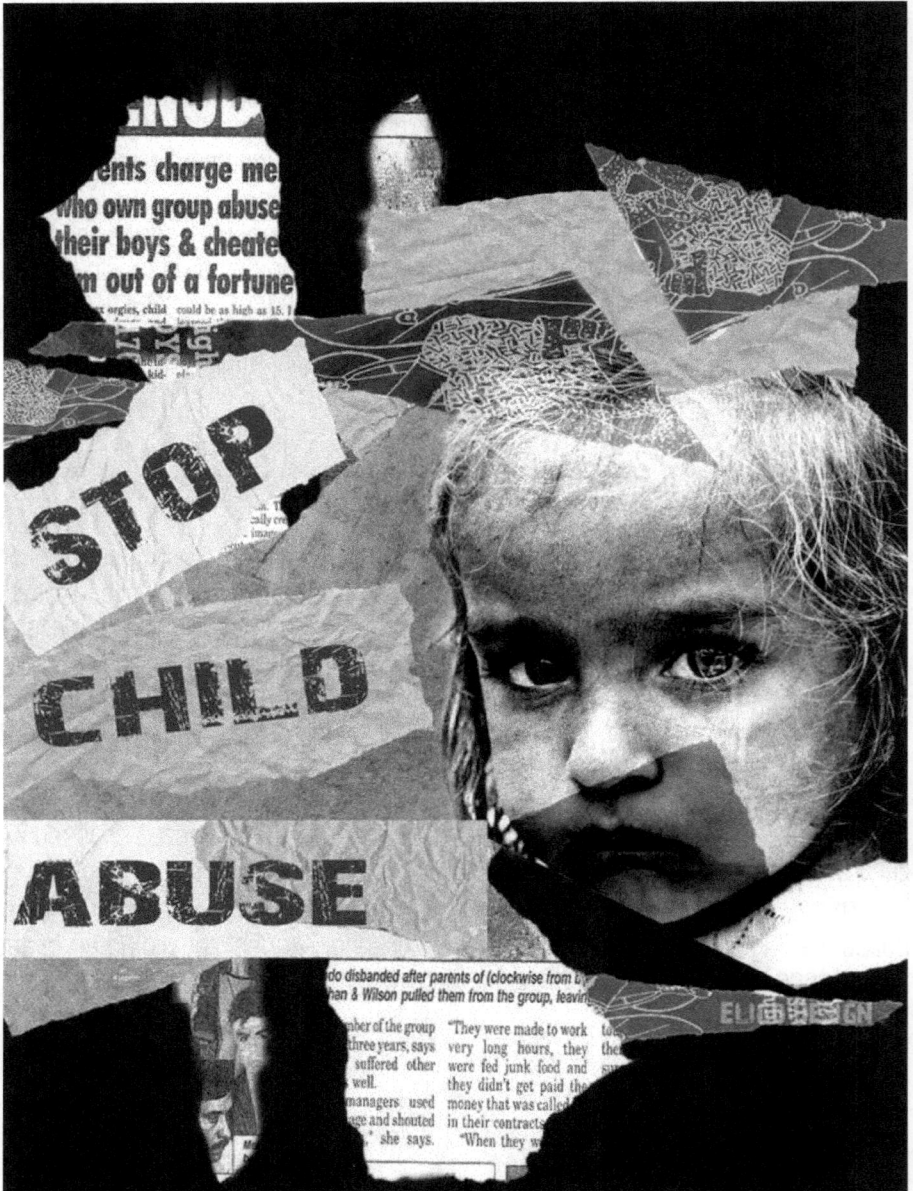

Frames

ancestral photo's hang.
spirits sleep here,
whispering on this soft air.
their auras surround
full exposures
                    of silent memories.

those lilliputian dressed feet,
reside under modern ankles now.
party dresses, pressed trousers,
those ties . . . leer from seaside cliffs,
coney island cavalcades,
                    and backyard vigils.

young man's cap
laced boots,
vests, and festive blouse.
he stands alone.
tall in creeping snow.
                    smile never departed.

specters of lingersome impression
see through afterlife veils
to quiet reserves
of living space,
not-so-white walls,
                    overwhelming art.

subtle thinness
of covert separation,
carry the moments.
naked folly residing over
bent shoulders - warped knees.
                    candles hued,

incensed native rites
stake claims.
strongholds,
fortitudes,
lasting reunions,
                    then relative and blanched futures.

imbued ascendant
now cherry ripened, lives
flushed sage,
housing melted minds,
an eternal consciousness,
            their randomized geniuses.

touching benefactors to aid,
rather message,
volumes obscured.
seeking generations,
their deliverance,
            and hoped for re-generations.

Families for Depression Awareness

Frames Back Story

As a young child, during a wonderful time of discovery, I visited my maternal

*Published in New Zealand's B l a c k m
a i l P r e s s 3, ISSN 1176-4791 in
March of 2002 – Guest Editor
Christina Conrad*

grandmother and grandfather's home in West Pittston, Pennsylvania for summers and holidays. Our grandparents resided on Linden Street near the Susquehanna River. Their home housed the Family Bible with full color images and stories of God, Jesus and Disciples; it also held vintage photos of family members from the far past.

There were a set of colonnades leading into the den from the living room. The colonnades housed porcelain teacups and shoes along with other collectibles. There were additional teacups in a China hutch in the dining room where an over-abundant dining table often held major amounts of home baked goods for the American Legion and other volunteer services Grandmother adored.

My sister and I often sat behind French glass-paned doors, which led from the den to the dining room, to play tea. We'd don fake faux stoles, hats and gobs of antique costume jewelry from Grandmother's jewelry chest to play tea-time while pretending we were British ladies at high noon. We also looked through familial gems housed in the Family Bible as well as glass-lined bookcase drawers, the piano bench, and other concealments. Our tea times were nothing less than heavenly. The brightest memories of playing with my sister stem from this era. It was always a journey visiting the Grand's for holidays and summer's extended vacations. And let's not get started on our investigations of their coal bin and chests of drawers housed nearby in the cellar. Those were true adventures . . . intrepid, scary and full of discovery.

Wyoming Ave. and Linden Street.
West Pittston, Pa.

Vintage photographs featured our Victorian Era Family and other folk, who had arrived in America from Germany, Scotland, Wales, and Ireland. All the grandfather(s), mother(s), aunt(s), uncle(s), cousin(s), and etc. were included. Notations were written in delicate inks with solid representation because our ancestors presumed we'd be reviewing their lives today. Among them was John Henry Naugle born in DArmstadt Hessen, Germany. He married one Katherine Elizabeth Conrad – daughter of John Conrad and Miss Dampman - born 26 July 1840 also in DArmstadt Hessen, Germany. Apparently, the two of them loved one another enough to have ten children. One of their children, August Conrad Naugle born 9 May 1873 in Pittston, Pennsylvania became our great-grand-father.

August determined to marry Grace Fisher Thompson, who had been born 6 June 1876; they married 7 June 1894 in Pittston and not so many years later . . . Grace passed away 22 July 1922. Being lonely, August remarried to one Bernice Hastie sometime thereafter. However, during their time together, August and Grace managed to have four children: Robert Thompson, Marian, Clinton August, and Edwin Thompson.

Robert, Marian and Edwin changed their last names to Nagle, while Clinton used Naugle. In photographs a reasoning for last name variations never presented itself and I recollect wondering, *Why?*

These early pioneers fought in the Civil War and descendants in World War(s) I and II. Yes, some were American Germans who fought the Germans during the War.

Love.Life.memories.............................

These images came to mind in one photograph of my Great Uncle Joe, who donned a spritely suit with knee high boots, jodhpurs and a vest with a white button up shirt. He stood stalwart as a youngster in fallen snow and continued to do so in life until his golden years. The "frames" back story originates from snapshots like his and the residual effects on the psyche of children and families who view them over time.

Tinged Bassinet — With Verbs

puerto rican
exposes his dirt pile
in brushed briars.
oh . . . virgin loss
with fears muffled
under his fleeced coat.
wrestlers pin delivered
slopped mouth drippings
of nippled bruises, and
leaf filled crevasse.

impasse - no awards.

desert boots skated down
glassy pasted hardwood
to that frigid landing.
being basement floored,
doped laughter, remained
chicken necked hideous.
belted parents, those
pubic inquest sentries,
raised lesions.
grade: diapered seven.

impasse - no escapes.

uncle festered his
little tittied cutesy,
past momma to
a modern turf.
sickened stomach, and
stoned smiled hostage.
high achiever, their
cipher stealthed lordette,
housed ulcerated bowels
remained . . . road kill pretty.

impasse - no communion.

Tinged Bassinet – With Verbs Back Story

A young girl twelve (12) years of age should find day-to-day living nonconsequential; at that age I did. Each day involved rising for school,

Published in New Zealand's B l a c k m
a i l P r e s s 3, ISSN 1176-4791 in
March of 2002 – Guest Editor
Christina Conrad

participating while there, studying, performing chores and playing with friends if all else was done. Our experience was upwardly mobile, in a selective neighborhood, nestled in the forest near a main thoroughfare. Parks, stores, shops, movies and all recreational venues were about ten minutes away in any given direction – with Washington DC only twenty minutes away in traffic at that time. McDonald's hadn't arrived in our community yet – it came about two years later and was still a ten-minute drive when it did arrive. We were safely tucked away just outside the city – close enough for a quick visit – far enough to enjoy life.

Our neighborhood had a one road in – one road out mentality; that is, unless you knew the farmer's road in the back, which no one really knew except extreme locals. There were one-half acre lawns for each home with heavy forestation, creeks and footpaths for play. And we did get about the neighborhood when we weren't doing chores. We used to swing across the creek on vines and play in the forest without worry.

Our mother was dedicated. She cooked full course meals with appetizers, salads, main courses, and desserts. We said a blessing at dinnertme and ate together as a family. If we weren't at the table eating our meal and finishing our plates, we'd be certain to be put on restriction where chores were the imperative word of the hour.

Mother kept our hardwood floors like mirrors. A slip at the top of the split foyer would projectile a guest right out the front door, like an ejection button. There were days you actually had to hold the wall to get up the hallway after a fresh paste and buff. Our home remained dust and clutter free. It was decorated well and we weren't allowed to introduce inappropriate items to be on display such as 1960's and early 1970's posters.

One season the Susquehanna River overflowed its banks; our grandparents had to emergency out of their home by powerboat. An Uncle, who lived with them at the time, had left them behind when they wouldn't leave with him. They knew they were losing all of their memories and had a hard time saying goodbye to their home. But they did. Those memories we had worked diligently to explore each summer as children and investigated in their cellar as shared in the "frames" back story were lost to the flood.

The majority of their home had held huge floral wallpaper with over-stated doorjamb ornaments – all also ruined by the flood. In the aftermath and recovery, the former Victorian era decorative devices were replaced with 1970's wood paneling, shag carpeting and new founded concepts of décor. All the Victorian fanfare was replaced with straight baseboard linings and the magic of their home was forever altered.

It was devastating for both of them. Our mother went to help with cleanup and was gone for many months. The mud that remained after the waters receded required scraping by the shovelfuls from the cellar and first floor. This was only one of a variety of post-flood clean-up requirements. The coal shaft was replaced by an electric furnace heat. The old stove with metal catches to lift griddles, was replaced with a modern electric version. The cabinetry was removed and replaced as well. The upper floors retained their former style to some degree but paneling made its way there too.

The former stair runner, an ornamental carpet, was replaced. The iron claw sunken bathtub continued to be functional; initially, the bathroom sink and medicine cabinet full of old powder remedies without labels we used to mix in water until a bubbling gruel arose remained intact; however, it was converted to modernity including contents of the medicine chest eventually. The pull handle toilet switched up too – even the attic door seemed to have new vigor. No more peering eyes from the attic as cousins shared the massive front room bed – it was well sealed now – and the raccoons or squirrels were none the wiser.

In Mother's absence, Father stayed behind in Southern Maryland managing us three children. School was very important to our parents and we weren't about to miss any of it. Due to this, my elder sister was largely the woman in charge. Chores were increased to compensate for Mother's absence. We two girls cooked meals and performed other duties Mother usually mitigated.

Apparently, too, my sister wasn't happy to be in charge. She ruled like a *Till of the Hun* and we fought. Clearly, we loved one another but she was four years older, just getting into boyfriend land. She was the second lead majorette for our high school and was naturally put out to have to step up to the home plate while Mother was away – this was a natural result. Father worked often because he ran a Real Estate office as a Broker and this was during the boom era when housing went from $8 to $12K and then jumped again from $30 and $40K and not long thereafter to $60 to $80K and so on and so forth.

Our father was a proper salesman. He was honest and had a good heart. The folks he helped into homes always returned during their home-buying years. He made houses affordable to blacks when it was difficult for them to acquire homes. I remember we would go visit folks he settled into homes and he would say, "I knew this man in the Air Force, he's a good man – he has a nice family."

Father had come from the Deep South originally and Mother from the North. We were a Mason Dixon family and all that entails – when amidst extended family it often appeared the Civil War had never ended, albeit the Northerners always appeared to be more openminded from my limited perspective as a child.

For Father, to aid blacks with housing after coming up in the South was truly a miracle. I was proud of him because the Civil Rights Movement was very declarative in our youth. Men died over equality when I was growing up. Father was a brave man, I believed privately.

During Mother's absence in Pennsylvania to aid my grandparents – I entered the first year of middle school in a new District. It wasn't considered as good a school as I attended the prior year. Father worked to get me into the former school District but the Board of Education said no. I made friends with blacks initially and was frowned on for not associating with just the white kids by other white kids. Schools had clicks: Preps, Heads, Grits and Blacks. Nerds came about in the late 1970's I believe but they were just considered pencil pushers then and not even on the radar.

Some Grits and a few Heads got to know me, which made school life a little easier. I'd never thought about boys to that point in time, I was a little girl. Whatever my sister did in the world of dating was a discussion between our parents and her. In fact, I just didn't see boys as anything other than basketball rivals or as partners in crime when investigating wildlife or swing-roping over the creek.

Suddenly, a fellow named Jack Radcliffe wanted to change all that and insisted on carrying my books etc. I had met Jack when I went to the horse farm to ride my horses . . . he lived across from the farm and had come over to introduce himself. Occasionally, he'd help me with moving bales of hay or holding lumber when tacking up stalls. He just laughed when I was cleaning stalls though . . .

I was flabbergasted by his suggestion to hold my books. So, when I was in my Home Economics class, I told my tablemate about this fellow who wanted to carry my books. She asked a lot of questions, which I thought were more interesting than normal but it appeared she wanted to know me and my story. I learned otherwise after school when she met me in the front lobby wanting to fight. Apparently, the boy who carried my books, my summertime assistant at the farm . . . was her boyfriend.

I was not one to fight anyone, except my sister and that was home turf close action battle of wits more than anything else – really never a fight per se. I'd never really fought with anyone to this point in time. This teenage girl, I was told later, had been held back a time or two. She threw off her jacket and did and said things totally foreign to me . . . I wasn't certain what to do or why we were at these cruxes of conversational fodder when a mild discussion would have served us both better. At least, I recollect thinking in those terms.

As she kept puffing out at me, like an animal beating its chest in overly aggressive bravado; I presumed her lunges were meant to ignite a response. Instead, I was dumbfounded. And being strong as a bull ox (Mother often said that to me) I was worried I might hurt her because I did haul 100 lb. bags of oats around routinely. I was equally worried this might be a weaponized version of humanity standing so oddly in front of me. I noted the front office was close in the distance and it would certainly not bode well with them. I hoped someone would come out due to the commotion but no one did.

During all this mental foreplay, she suddenly she stopped and grew silent. I felt a crowd gathered behind me and presumed they were there to observe the battle; however, one of my black friends' brother spoke up . . . "If you want to fight Donna, you'll be fighting all of us," he'd called out. And, then about two hundred black friends said in unison, "That's right, you'll be fighting us too."

She turned and walked away in a dramatic fashion. I was never as happy as that day, realizing my ideals on friends were spot on. Friends didn't come in colors – then came in qualities. My black friends I'd been bullied for engaging, saved the day when no one else would have. The boy who had carried my books said he could not put me in jeopardy any longer and he continued dating his former girlfriend. They were too advanced for me anyhow – already sexually active and the like. Sadly, Mr. Jack Radcliffe passed away early in life from complications from cancer and his younger brother committed suicide.

My other "newer" friends, who were Heads, not long afterward asked me to go Christmas shopping at the local mall. It was situated just outside Southeast DC in Suitland, Maryland and was the place to go to shop in the early 1970's. Mother had just returned home from being away for so many months. I asked my Father if I could go to the mall with the only White friends, I had at that time . . . the Heads. The ex-combatant was a Grit and they stopped talking with me after our encounter. Father said, "Yes – you can go." My Mother said, "No." I pleaded with my daddy and won. My parents were living a strained reawakening at the time, and I was inadvertently putting it to my advantage and later blamed for taking them at a disadvantage but I was only twelve at the time. I know now that is what twelve-year-olds do, having raised five of my own.

When we went to the mall the group took me to the nearby recreational center. There were two of my schoolmates and their sister and brother from High School who drove. My parents thought their parents were driving, as did I, until we got into the car. The eldest, kept talking about smoking pot, which I didn't want to do. She continuously stated how cool it was and how everyone had to try it . . . suggesting it would loosen me up and make me less anxious about living life. I guess I seemed uptight to them as a kid.

When we arrived at the center, their pot dealer showed up and they began smoking weed. Everyone insisted I give it a puff – it was the early 1970's after all – sex, drugs and rock n' roll as it were. I learned my classic pot smoking dupe at that time. The dupe served me well whenever a need to smoke presented itself. I just breathed a little into my mouth, held it and then blew it out. Over the years, I got this down to an Oscar winning performance as I never really grew fond of pot smoking but folks who did felt more comfortable if I appeared to be on their playing field when they lit up a joint. It just alleviated pain points to act as if I smoked too.

With their smoking put aside – my friends all departed. They left me with the dealer fellow and said they'd be right back. I was not comfortable with their decision but didn't really know where we were having not been to the recreational center previously. I hadn't paid close attention walking to the rec center from the mall. I just shrugged, wanting to keep the evening moving in forward motion and grew anxious to be back safe at home.

Once they left, the fellow decided to try and kiss me. I'd only kissed one boy prior to that in fifth grade and this is while our friends were giving instructions on, "How to kiss" like movie stars. At the time, it seemed sort of similar to taste testing food, which was not pleasant. Since he wasn't gaining ground with kissing me as I wasn't very compliant, he suggested we move to an opening under the bushes where it appeared folks sat from time-to-time. He stated he heard someone coming and that it could be police who would know they'd all just smoked pot; he motioned for us to hide there.

Reluctantly, I went. And I no more than sat down, the man was on top of me sucking on my face as if it was the last hope for oxygen. He tore at my shirt and jeans. He pulled my shirt off and ripped at my training bra. The ground was dirty, rocky and cold. He started telling me I was going to love what was about to happen. I wrestled to free myself and my hair got stuck in the brambles of the bushes – I later learned he had been a high school wrestler. He pinned me and then shoved his penis into my vagina. With it was gravel, rocks, dirt and fallen leaves – some twigs too. He began thrusting and gripped my arms over my head while sucking on my neck, which became reddened and then purple. I remember him saying, "They'll see that I better suck lower." He continued this pattern of sucking and biting at me until my breasts, abdomen and stomach were bruised. I was trying to scream and he put a hand over my mouth, which he replaced with his parka.

He kept saying, "You know you like this, you know you like this." He just kept on saying it. As I got more and more violent in struggling to free myself, he pressed harder and harder. Under the parka I could hardly breathe. I remember debris rubbing my skin and the pain of his sucking and biting and thrusting and the brambles now broken into my hair and scrapes on my scalp and feeling punched in the vagina. As I screamed, I stretched my head out from under his overbearing body to gasp for air. He smashed the parka over my face even harder and I resolved not to fight any longer.

At the time, I didn't understand what sex was. I presumed what happened was what people do to have sex. My supposed friends were all congratulatory afterward, as if I'd just won an award. I was petrified but acted the part of the awardee. What I wanted to do was to go home, get into my room and lock the door. The fellow continued to act as if he just made love to me. He acted as if I were his new pet and I mustered up a good old elementary school take one for the team demeanor by trying to act cool.

So that's sex I remember thinking to myself, *Why do people do that?* I wondered because it seemed dirty (literally dirty), awkward, painful and made no sense to me.

The friends drove me home and we were late. Everyone was angry. I was met with, "Where have you been?" at my parents' front door. It was obvious someone had defiled me, with a purple neck, bruised face, debris all over, mussed up hair, dirty clothing. My father said to my mother, "Check her and see . . ."

Mother took me to my room and made me strip out of my jeans for an examination, she yelled out, "Yes . . . someone got her." It was much like when a dog jumped the fence for our French poodles to my recollection when Mother checked to see if they'd been violated. I now realized how Tinkerbell and Lady felt.

My Father then came to my room and pulled me to the rec room. With his Air Force belt, he beat me until blood blisters formed on my legs and thighs. He told Mother to take me upstairs and scrub me. She pulled me up the stairs and filled the tub with scalding hot water. She got a scrubbing pad and had me step into the tub.

It was too hot, I jumped back out. She shoved me back in and began scrubbing me until I was reddened and raw. All the while she continued to say, "No man is ever going to think you are a pretty girl ever again." She then got out the long sheers and began to hack off my hair in clumps. She furthered, "I never liked this hair anyway . . ." She ripped out my pierced earrings while saying, "Enough of that nonsense, you shouldn't have pierced your ears — you're gonna listen now little girl."

Father called the police and drove me to the stationhouse in Upper Marlboro. I was stripped naked once more and given a paper sheet, then placed on a metal table with sinks and saws and weird apparatuses nearby. The doctor saw my welts and asked, "Where did those come from?"

"My Father spanked me." I answered him.

He retorted, "Probably served you right."

Later, I was redressed and sat in front of two detectives who questioned me for what seemed like hours. I barely understood half the things they said to me. It was some time afterward; I had to go to court and didn't understand any questions presented to me there either. They spoke of copulation and coitus and intercourse. I just kept saying, "I don't know what that means."

The Detective's doctor insisted I wasn't a virgin, so I was donned a "slut" throughout my youth after that night. Today, I know the summer prior, while bike riding when the front tire slipped into a slat on the wooden bridge, and the seat drove up inside my vagina it removed my hymen. But at the time, I didn't even know what a hymen was except for in sex education classes, which didn't really convey to real life. After the bike accident, I went to Mother and told her the bike seat had impaled me and made me bleed — she never said anything to me about it and didn't explain why this happened. I remember worrying I'd cut myself inside but she just said, "You're okay — go play."

And the fact I took the sex education class twice, so I could go to my friend's classroom for the 1.5-hour presentation had not boded well either. Apparently, I was a "sexy girl" who couldn't get enough sex education. But no one realized my best friend and I had discussed our plan for me to take it twice in order to visit – we paid little attention to the actual program at the time.

For years after the rape, extended male relatives felt it was okay to molest me. At least one uncle did, and a number of cousins. The older cousin said, "Well, you done given up the goods now girl, there's nothing left to worry about – the damage has already been done." I fought him off, kicking the door open after he refused to drive me to my Aunt's home in South Carolina when my other cousin baled on me on Main Street where we rode back and forth from Tasty Freez to the fire station as a form of entertainment. This cousin was an adult man, a cousin to my father who said, "You remind me of my first wife – she fought like a hell cat too." I hit him in the face with my clogs and scratched him too before running down the gravel road he'd driven to in my bare feet. I ran until they bled attempting to get away. When I fell in exhaustion, praying to God for him to save me, he grabbed my hair from behind and pulled me to my knees. As I kept pleading for God to help me, he responded, "I wouldn't harm a hair on your head darling. Get up. I'll drive you home. Don't worry I won't touch you."

Thank God for Southern men's sensibilities when it comes to God and prayer.

Later in time my Uncle, at his house party for military retirement, grabbed my breast while passing me on the stairwell. One of his Air Force buddies was following him down the stairs. Both men were of high enough rank to know better. They chuckled as if it was hysterical to grab the breast of a young teen-ager.

Over time, I learned not to share issues like these with my parents. Invariably it was my fault. I once asked Mother if she believed I was ruined after the rape. She answered. "Well, you were ruined. You are ruined now." And my father spat at my feet a few times when he was irritated; he was always reminding me, "People are going to think you're a slut" if I wanted to have a boyfriend at school – so I didn't.

It was easiest to let go when those sorts of events occurred and just to act as if they never happened. However, Mother didn't mean I was ruined as a human being . . . she meant rape ruined my innocence. And Father didn't mean to be cruel but his own inner demons surfaced. That Deep South mentality he worked so hard to discard would riddle his otherwise calm and modern demeanor every now and again. While not feeling these were appropriate coping mechanisms – because they were not – it is a reality in the 1970's, a sexual assault victim was blamed and treated harshly by even those who loved them the most. It was, at that time, not necessarily the fault of the loved ones for doing so, as it was the standard cultural trait of the era but it did little to help me grow into healthy relationships in the future.

In recent years, during regressive hypnosis, I grew to understand my parents who dealt poorly with my having been brutally raped, were scared themselves. They were innocent as adults, in an era of severe transition. They wanted the best for their children. The rapist soiled their dreams. Everything they'd worked for was jeopardized. In regressive hypnosis, I saw them in the moments of tragedy but could not re-visit that particular event – it was too painful. I did discover my parents' inability to process the situation and their shock . . . it was palpable. Their feelings of loss and betrayal were as well. And I experienced my sister's attempts to dissuade them from overreacting and her own feelings, which were pain-stricken.

When a rapist perpetrates their crime – it is perpetrated on not only the individual they attack – it is also an attack on families, friends, and community. Sexual assault has generational repercussions. My innocence was not only stolen from me but also my parents and siblings and friends and community lost their innocence too.

In regressive hypnosis, I saw Father, Mother; Sister and Brother as harmless attempting to digest a tragic event. They were each striving in the post-50's, 60's and early-70's with a "Leave it to Beaver" familial mindset suddenly plummeted into an apocalyptic nightmare. *Leave It to Beaver* children weren't raped. I was raped. And it instantly resulted in our no longer living an episodic life of bliss and joy – evil had crept in.

In every other way, both Father and Mother were exceptional parents. As long as I presented no problems, studied, got good grades, rode my horses and behaved – life was good – so that is what I did. We eventually recovered but never spoke about the fact I was sexually assaulted. Throughout the years – even to this day – we do not discuss it.

Love.Life.memories.................................

In "tinged bassinet with verbs," the wrongfulness of sexual assault is what I was striving to deliver. It wasn't so much about my own situation as the universal reality rape results in lifelong devaluation of the victim. While not prejudiced, the assault I sustained was by a Puerto Rican man and I shared the line, "exposes his dirt pile" to signify the depth of indignation I feel today concerning his act at the time. I hold no issue with the Puerto Rican culture, and really feel leaving that statement in sets a tone I rarely present in writing, as I hold a certain disdain for racial slurs and stereotypes. It was "hard" for me to include the line in this work.

When family and friends have no prior experience regarding disaster recovery and management of human nature – it is a stark reality. Hardship is difficult to relate to when it has remained avoidable through a lifetime. For me, sexual assault became a horrid facet of my personal composition. And, in our family, it was something everyone wanted to forget.

But . . . like the pink elephant in the room . . . the albatross of having been raped was eternally collared above my shoulders.

Over time, I've discovered trauma is not an easy pill to swallow. Everyone approaches abuse, assault, and violence in their own way. In the heat of the moment, during heightened emotion, and extreme episodic feelings of intensity, humankind appears far less than human. Certainly, my parents were normal parents every other day of our youth because once adrenalin subsides and rational thought prevails, over-reaction is very often replaced with a contrite heart and spirit . . . this was the case in my family.

It should go without saying, I also wrote this poem, and shared this story, as a cathartic exercise concerning wrongful secrets regarding early-life traumas many families hide from public scrutiny. Healing involves recognition in order to recover and move forward. To let go of the past – one must set it free. This personal nightmare of my youth is now freed . . . thank you for reading it with me thereby removing another bar from the cage around my soul.

Decorated Tenant

labial retentive
his gaze was
a compilation
of ploys in leisure
suits of leather
thinking this
the savored lining
of his proverbial

silk purse
to lie on his mantle
of metal fixtures
sterile | motionless
when all it
required was:

a spit shine
a buff
a nutriment
and poise

Decorated Tenant Back Story

Printed in *Meeting of the Minds Journal* in 2004.

This poem aligns to repressed sexuality and the reality men not only repress — they are often repressed too. As I grew toward womanhood through marriages, birthing, divorcement and late-life dating (something I'd not been able to do pre-marriage), I began observing emotions and/or the lack of feelings many men espoused toward women they supposedly cared for.

In "decorated tenant" the woman serves as proverbial arm candy, while the man remains indebted as it were to the essence of womanhood. Hence, his labial retentive posturing.

To deal with this truth — it appeared men or this man — would underscore reasons for preoccupations with women in a controlled guise so as to not upset their posturing regarding what they often viewed as weaknesses. And, in certain eras of time, a man and men in general, would swallow swords before professsing love toward the women in their lives except in some cultura deviations where professing love towards mothers and wives was iconic. Still, even among these cultures, such professions were mocked. To avoid appearing weak by their need for love — men often categorized women. This is representatior of a sterile mindset housing images on a metal mantle of reverence, which is shackled by its cold, austere, placement in the man's life.

In this work, the woman who seemingly just needed a little nurturing is presented as equally skewed and therefore pained while portraying a seemingly advanced state of propriety. In gaining poise, decision-making transitions to the female, who accepts and rejects simultaneously. Her emotive game-playing is virtually the same as the man's opposing guise. And, in this is a level of melancholy, I attempted to wield in this work.

Love.Life.memories.................................

As a survivor of sexual assault and domestic violence, an underscore of total non-involvement is often experienced by survivors such as I regarding past abuse, assault and violence. Superficially engaged in a relationship, with or without an underlying desire for true love, a measure of survivor mentality remains permanently etched in the psyche of the soul. This results in detachment. No matter the disguise of sterile un-involvement or earthbound lack of requirement – the result is the same – extrication or disconnection hidden by aloofness.

Both of these emotional underpinnings are equally harmful. Either debilitates an individual's ability to attain their hierarchy of needs. While the man in this work projects sterility and emotional disengagement, the woman does also. Her lack of desire actually compliments his lack of presence. The result is two people who actually harmonize with one another through not being charitable toward one another.

It was my intent to share the turmoil of broken emotions and the fact they affect both individuals, while each would believe theirs' to be an appropriate strategy toward independent health and wellness. Abuse and violence attached to interpersonal relationships results in lifelong struggles. These are often impossible to overcome. "décorated tenant" demonstrates this truth.

Your Congress

your congress enjoined with my parts today—
parts time has
          decided
                    will belay your vision into my depths

sunlight hid itself in a cloud lined ceiling—
lined with silver plated
            reality
                    capturing the gray matter of my cortex

life's beat strode hard, passed the church—
the steeple, metal spires
            drove
                    an extra pulsation and flow of my vein

dusk again, set upon the horizon gathering
melting into the dank
            obscurity
                    sleep's revelry prevails on my anatomy

your congress may again enjoin with mine tomorrow—
mine is the soothsayer's
            future
                    god's simple pleasures in us a coupling.

Your Congress Back Story

Working in the city, I used to take lunch and go to Catholic Cathedrals to meditate. At the time, I wanted to believe the act of love held a Godliness, which

*Printed in Spyder's Poetry Empire in
2003; also won a separate poetry
award in 2004.*

provided clarity we all, and I mostly, needed.

There were a few years in writing where I focused on love, relationships, and acceptance of sexuality and human nature. Having experienced violence in the first sexual act put upon my person, viewed by loved ones and the perpetrator as an act of lovemaking; it became apparent to me, early in life, sexual congress (as it is often ascribed in legal texts) or the conjoining of two physical bodies is often overlooked as a spiritual union. I believe the ideal of entering another human being's body should have merit worthy comprehension, weight of consideration, and a certain ethereal respect. Yet, it appeared to me at that time, the consequence of joining a sexual union alluded to most everyone as anything more than a handshake. Which too, I'd felt was worthy of greater weight than provided even today.

In defining the spiritual union – I denoted a preponderance of architectural structures, art forms, clichés and many - social memes shared through time. Systemic on base levels, regarding the union of spirits, souls and bodies; the only moments of deference to these obvious symbols remained within the realm of lucidness where life ebbs into the ether allowing the sprit and soul and body to rest in calm. Even furniture has maintained a very phallic nature in context and design.

In a delightful way, the spiritual, physical and soulful union is a simple pleasure we tend to over complicate by clouding it with mental hang-ups and angst but not at the very least identifying with the source of all unions – the

Godhood and the religion of the human soul — otherwise results in a disingenuous story of life, expressly in the sexual arena.

Each new day offers a new simplicity, as we all conjoin in the bounty that is life in an act of love.

Love.Life.memories............................

"your congress" shares a story concerning the visionary aspect of joining two souls engaging supra-physical appetites rather than fleshly ones.

Wr.tng

wrote about myself once
re-read it years later,
a pretentious piece,
should've been edited . . .
that girl,
somewhere inside me,
while i may not like her now

i still love her

"poor thing"

Poetry and prose can be so self-serving.

Who do we write for?

Oftentimes, we write for ourselves. Other times, many write to prove a point where the only one truly listening is themselves. Many survivors of child abuse, sexual assault, and domestic violence write poetry. It is an emetic measure to take back what is stolen through torture, aggression, mental anguish, physical pain and suffering.

Why should anyone read about the least profound declarations of the poet who is learning to make reflective statements? There's almost a self-inflicted humor in the matter of writing poetry on so many levels.

A young fellow who dated a daughter of mine, once told me, in reference to four news columns I wrote, "Who wants to know what you think anyhow? Who the hell are you?" In some ways, he was absolutely correct. "Who the hell am I?" I guess we are all trying to discover that extremely one-dimensional question and each of us hope it matters, at the very least, to one other human being beside ourselves.

Then, it came to me, well – I came to think – I do love myself even in my weakest form. And, yes, some unfortunate poems and prose are frail, so the weak or the strong might weep with me, which has absolutely nothing to say about the merit of my work. Many a poet's weakest days are someone else's strongest.

But it is good to not self-import oneself to the point of losing ourselves or perhaps loosing ourselves is of the greatest importance. It is paradoxical.

Love.Life.memories...........................

In this work, I bore a vantage point that some of my earliest writs were ascribed to the mindset of self-flagellation. As healing journeys, thrashing our words appear as selfish acts. In re-reading my earliest poems, I find them droll and patronizing - even pompous in their overly forlorn presentation; however, at the time – those were true feelings, which assuaged my transcendence from abuse and violence as well as the residual ectoplasm called violence.

This poem carries the double-entendre of being a device for emotional healing and also exploitative narcissism. One is needed to heal; the other is the result of preoccupation with conflict. Self-love is after all, the only cure for ruinous histories.

There are times when both are evident and make for good sense; however, in the process of restoration of the human psyche, I believe a survivor reaches a point where they realize somewhere along the path of recovery, they became poets with a consciousness readers share. It is then, the survivor transitions to the carrier of message for readers, rather than be purveyors of the exodus of angst shedding the pain they'd grown to entertain in the past. "wr.tng" encapsulates this for me in a few words, which are meant to be a few words.

In life, it's come down to just a few words as a recoveree from the many words abuse, assault and violence entail – even if uttered in silence.

Crafted Artistry and Hewed Woods

remembering   amsterdam
he opens the buffet
shuffling viennese linens.

she'd smiled   hardest
in her shortest skirts,
his attention allowed to focus.

lace cloth   tucked under elbow,
he gathers a water lily vase
in compliment to her,

and crosses the   terrace.
fichus trees cast vestal images
through wooden blinds.

buffing   furnishings,
he sets accoutrements
on a formal chair.

butter almond english   balm
moves through the rooms
with resilience.

hands   steady.
he holds them
in front of his eyes.

his   skin,
his   veins,
his   lean fingers,

manicured spoils of   labor.
he sets a cloth aside
to draw water.

washing to   elbows,
a bar of lavender soap
he holds close to his nose.

whiffing   sensations.
water echoes
as vapors rise.

immersion's his   temptation.
he turns, checks a burner
and adjusts a dial,

unfolding the   lace cloth
sets it on rich wood,
replaces his spectacles.

begins a   new chapter.
waits in silence.
remembers she forgot her scarf.

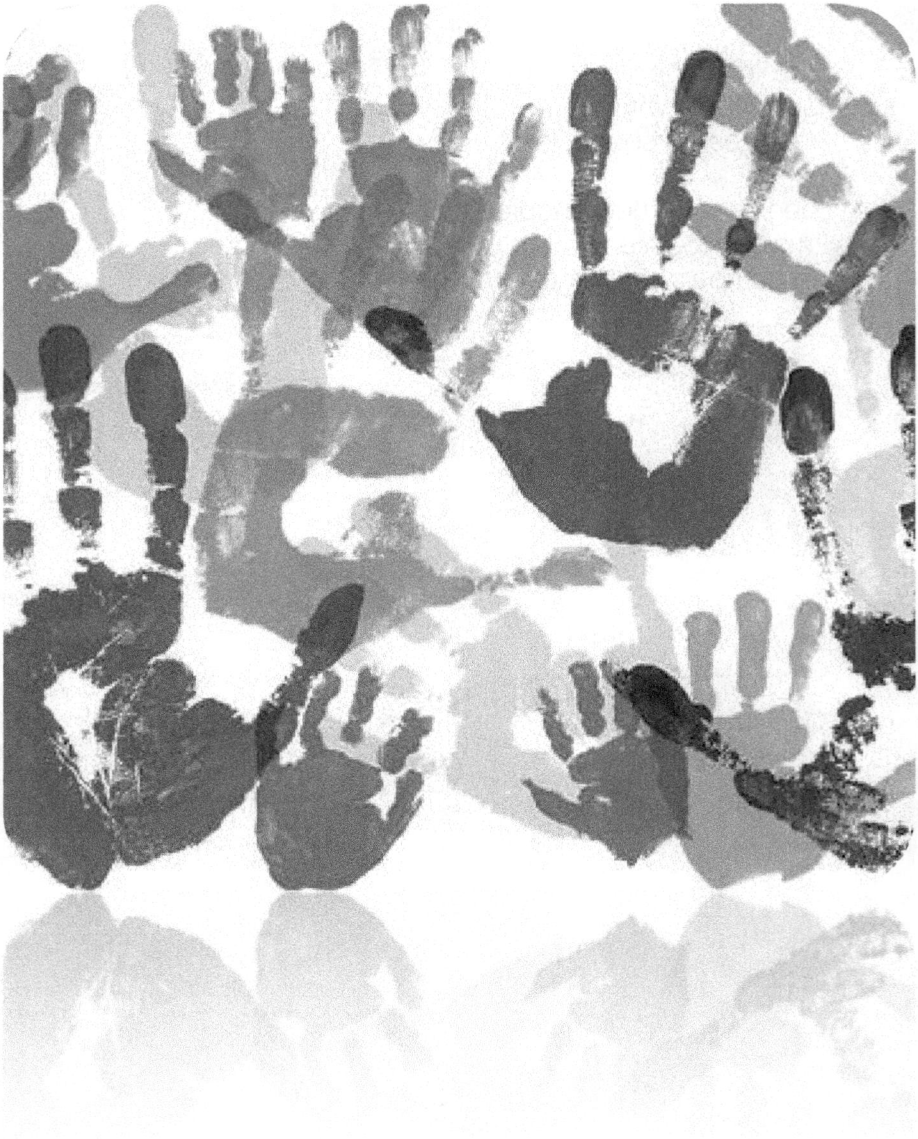

Crafted Artistry and Hewed Woods Back Story

Shared on "The Poet's Lament" in 2009 with good reviews.

In an era of life, I'd grown to have a strong affinity for Eastern European cultures. Studying through the Smithsonian Resident Associate's program at Meridian House in Washington, DC many unique personalities came to bare but for some reason the Eastern European community sought me out before that time. I can remember as far back as grade school, meeting my first friend from Europe.

While Slavic people are often portrayed in movies as impoverished or as crime lords . . . the fact is Eastern Europeans involve many countries with as many variations of individuals as any other country. In my experiences, I've found men from these nations have shared good manners toward me. They have tended to have unusual engagement practices – fairly old school – such as no public displays of affection, holding the door, and waiting for months to become sexually inclined.

Many Eastern European men like to date, have a sense of formality in doing so, and extend rather pleasantly refreshing behaviors. And I do remain an extremely patriotic citizen of the United States, with a strong loyalty to the men and women in uniform serving our nation. I did grow to love my Slavic friends through their proprieties. After all, with German, Scot, Welsh and Irish heritage, it is in my blood to have an affinity for persons from those regions of the world. And, in recorded history the Slavs would have been our neighbors.

Again, while studying at Meridian House in Washington DC, our Seminar instructors included interesting scholars such as David Gergen who was a White House adviser to four U.S. presidents including: Nixon, Ford, Reagan and Clinton. Also, foreign diplomats such as Yugoslavian Minister Milosevic who provided presentations. Milosevic, I recollect, expressed how the "motherland" was going to redefine Yugoslavia and then in the years that followed went on to do just that. I reflected on his declaration and felt it was somewhat obscene. It was purely radicalized in nature, not as a physical allocation we often ascribe to the poor word choice. He stood and declared they were going to War and they did. Members applauded and toasted and consumed foods afterwards – Meridian House was quite a thrill – and I wondered why someone wasn't calling someone to make a report and to brazenly say, "No!" But it wasn't that kind of party.

At any rate, at these events I remained classically aloof with a few conversational interludes and observed the goings-ons. I realized some of the men who were elder, had women on their arms in a season of life where they finally learned the tenor of their own voice. They peered into these ladies' eyes with genuine emotion from their soul. It was unmistakable as to who was immensely in love with their companions and who were merely entertaining causes of money or power or obligation.

About this same time frame, I loved to dance – alone – with partners of course but independently. I maintained a standoffish nature and shared minimal conversation at entrances to clubs, upper decks and while leaning over rails observing the crowds below. I'd identify good dancing partners and engage them in the freedom of tripping the light fantastic. As a dance aficionado derived from "Saturday Night Live" and the hustle era, I nestled in a few good years of active dancing at some of the city's nicest clubs at least one or two evenings a month as a form of therapeutic release post-divorcement as a single-mother of five children. And I managed a rule of arriving and leaving alone. I never felt the club was a place to start a romance.

While in these arenas, I also observed many men who were with women in the daytime seemingly in love and then, there they were at after hour events with men. These were extremely handsome men, with classic females in the daylight, who transitioned to gay men after one or two a.m. when the only club left open was a classic ballroom where great music played until the sun rose in the morning. It was a curious occasion to see the most handsome men in town, who had been with the most stunning women in town wining and dining . . . now dancing with other equally handsome men in the wee hours of the morn. They recognized me too and it was a quiet understanding everyone was going to remain quiet about the aberrations from day to night.

Love.Life.memories...............................

About this time, I began "crafted artistry," a few years later I refined it. The man in the story is a combination of men from Europe who demonstrated qualities I had only seen previously in grandfathers and great uncles directly from, or one generation removed from, their European roots. Those men had proprieties and weren't about to assault anyone. It also involves the activities I'd viewed over time and the juxtaposition of the two.

Over the years I thought too, how true love I've observed often includes a partner who just doesn't "get it." On very few occasions in life, we do share genuine ardor. Usually, one individual loves the most, and the other has less of a concept regarding what they share. I'm not certain it is not too cliché' to depict sentiment in this work. The fact is the man in the poem is ever-watchful and loving. He maintains his love without the ill effect of loving too much, and without the folly of disavowing heartfelt sentiment to save face.

Instead, he waits . . .

The character knows the truth of loving a woman who loves him a little less — maybe it is "he" who loves himself a little less but in knowing the truth of it, there is liberty. He loves all the more because his knowledge of the depth of his understanding drives him to.

While he alone recognizes the cognizance of his love, it will never allow him to be alone because it is love's very nature that draws in more while it releases. Without struggle, or ill will, these characters are pieces of personalities viewed in these façades.

Speak Out Against Sexual Assault
Every voice counts. Every story matters.

She Spoke With Aquinas, He Told Her

To Go Home, To Wait

◇◇◇◇◇◇

crossed earth
grabbing dreams
putting them in parcels
to send back home

~~~~~~~~~~~~

opened tabloids
countering ills
packaged them for shelf
images to store forever

~~~~~~~~~~~~

discovered mysteries
escapist visionary renderings
holding auras captive
in every space saying vacancy filled

◇◇◇◇◇◇

She Spoke With Aquinas Back Story

Shared and refined on William (Billy Marshall Stoneking) Randolph Marshall-Stoneking's Performance Poetry through the former Suite101.com

Life gives. We take. At times, we share. Often, we put the light of life in a quiet place so on cloud-lined days we can escape to where the light once shone.

What about the light of being? Is it conceptually viable to capture auras? And, if they rock us, is it our right to do so . . . contain them for personal agglomerations? Is this what we do in affirmations, which the world loves today? Are we affirming or capturing futures through aural spin-cycles?

A curious consideration . . . in our dream state . . . do we really dream for ourselves? Do our dreams belong to us or is even our subconscious working to achieve the goals of others? Is the ecosphere of our reverie a natural state or an environmentally learned state? What about the collective wavelength of unconsciousness ~ is it designed to ebb and flow to its own unveiling . . . are personages afterthoughts of intellect?

In the wellspring of imaginings, is it possible a stock inventory of repertoire is part and participle of existence itself? How many ideations does the silenced mind conjure in one lifetime? What about the world's lifetime? Does humanity accumulate its richest experiences for the universal minds' sleep state? Are we warehousing synapses and their voices for safekeeping? Are those otherworldly calculators tallying up the sum totals of fantastic masterpieces any of us might achieve, and then closing the floodgate when we've had our fill or quota of vision quests?

Dreams and then translucence of secrets, are they our truest creations? Is this why they appear to be packaged, shelved and stored in our minds? Is the secret giver using our storekeeper to their own avail? Do we take these intangible treasures into eternity? And, if we gather a certain quota of oeuvres – is life's clock acknowledging and saying – you've reached maximum privileges in the quietness of your mind? Is it then that we go home meeting the end of our personal destination in this estate of living?

aquinas thought not – instead he said, "settle down and make things last – wait," because aquinas was a visionary.

love.life.memories.............................

Formally, aquinas (the muse of this work) was an Italian Dominican friar and Catholic priest. He was also an influential philosopher and theologian in the tradition of scholasticism. He is often referred to as Doctor Angelicus and Doctor Communis.

He is the father of Thomism and the foremost classical proponent of natural theology. His influence on Western thought is considerable, and much of modern philosophy was conceived in the development or opposition of his ideas, particularly in the areas of ethics, natural law, metaphysics, and political theory. Unlike many currents in the Church of the time, Thomas embraced several ideas put forward by Aristotle — whom he referred to as the Philosopher — and attempted to synthesize Aristotelian philosophy with the principles of Christianity. According to Aquinas

> *". . . all acts of virtue are prescribed by the natural law: since each one's reason naturally dictates to him to act virtuously." But if we speak of virtuous acts, considered in themselves, i.e., in their proper species, thus not all virtuous acts are prescribed by the natural law: for many things are done virtuously, to which nature does not incline at first; but that, through the inquiry of reason, have been found by men to be conductive to well living."*

For this poem the artwork is, of course, precedent to the writ but what if the Virgin Mary herself spoke to aquinas? He'd tell her to go home, to wait, to rely on nature to provide her answers.

love.life.memories.............................

Again, as a survivor of domestic violence, sexual assault and child abuse the inability to cross earth and grab onto emotions – rather to package them to send home – speaks volumes of the shell of the post-trauma psyche.

A trauma survivor feels ripples of experiences throughout their life and ascribes them to eternal flights of consciousness. Wheels might touchdown long enough to gather some souvenirs but never long enough for moss to grow. There is safety in the constant motion of flight – it is effectually a safe harbor. The survivor does want to live on visionary renderings aquinas shares, which ascribe a commonsense practicality that in itself may be freeing.

However, as a survivor of abuse, assault and violence . . . staying in one place very long isn't viewed as freedom.

Survivors rarely find safety in the arms of practicality either. The fight or flight remains in the "on" position. The thinking ascribed to the philosophy of aquinas is actually an act of autonomy survivors require but it is most difficult to achieve.

Recoverees of abuse, assault, and violence see life in reversals. What is freedom to them is complacency to others. The act of "to go home to wait" is an impossibility. It is akin to driving conceptual nails as concepts. It is an activity difficult to achieve for many but dramatically more difficult for survivors . . . the act of contentment ascribes to a certain sense of comfort. Until liberated from the tentacles of their past traumas, most survivors view the calm of relaxation of day-to-day living as a dangerous undertaking. Give the survivor skydiving, parachuting, train hopping, sword play or firing ranges and they'll achieve. Give them a quiet evening at home and they'll fold.

SPEAK OUT

STOP
CHILD ABUSE!

White Walled Haripines

wanted to line these walls
with his essence.

p ainted them pure white.

wanted to skirt the circumference
with trellised roses.
p oured an ornate gravel walk.

wanted to polish the silver
with recognizable fanfare.
p urchased standard ware instead.

all i wanted went with the p .

White Walled Haripines Back Story

*Printed in Contemporary International
Poetry through Poetry Repairs.com.*

Marriage.

The original meme after mortality struck men and women in the Garden of Eden.

In considering marriage initially, an undercurrent ideal of an avenue toward freedom was ignited for me. Then I learned — it has its own *white walled haripines*.

For us, my first husband and I, the path of marital bliss after vows was scary. After our "I do's" and the familial festivities, our drive to the Appalachian Mountains for our honeymoon included hours of absolute and utterly confounding silence. Neither of us say nay a word.

Yes . . . liberty had come to this. It wasn't death but it wasn't emancipation either.

Certainly, we both knew this was not a lifetimes' endeavor. We knew sitting in our silence. It was just us for now but what did that mean?

We were liberated! The conquistadors set us free . . .

Overnight, we went from ineptitude to key decision makers.

As I write this as a single, much older adult, it is stating the obvious regarding the decrees we accomplished. And, for me, it was twice the trials and outcomes. In actuality, it is funny to say, I married twice, annulled once and divorced three times, which is a declarative frame for thinking in itself. I won't share the answer to that riddle today.

However, I will say, with marriage number two, it was my goal to achieve . . . everything depicted in white walled haripines. Husband number two, I met less than eighteen (18) months after husband number one marriage ended.

Number two, was a state wrestling champion, a military man (USMC), and very logistical. He had a high IQ and was handsome – as was my first husband. He adopted my eldest son, we married a year after meeting, and then we were shipped off to Hawaii to Kaneohe Air Station.

All the reasons I grew to love him became all the reasons to leave him later in life. He was logistical. He was a wrestler. And I learned all too well if I wasn't logistical – he'd wrestle me into submission. And, if that didn't work, he'd knock me around or pick me up and twist an ankle while I was seven months pregnant until he broke a toe and sprained or broke the bones holding the toes.

But . . . like many women and men who suffer domestic violence – I made my bed and felt I had to sleep in it. After all, if I hadn't asked to go to the mall the dreadful night I was raped, it would have never happened. If it hadn't had happened, extended family wouldn't have felt I was fair game for further molestation and violence, as it was said, "You are already ruined goods . . . why not?" Had I not insisted in marrying the only teenager I dated at seventeen years of age, I wouldn't have been the only divorcee in our family at age eighteen (18) and then newly married again at nineteen (19). I truly couldn't be the only divorcee twice over before I was twenty-five (25) years old, could I?

Instead, I hunkered down and became the wife of all seasons. A formidable homemaker. Cooking from dawn until dusk. Making fresh bread daily. Sewing children's clothes to save money. Keeping a spotless home with one, two, three, then four and finally five children. Making certain the wee sprites kept out of daddy's way after work so as to not stir him to anger and violent attacks on them, which I would then have to deter me, which was a dance with fire each occasion.

Not leaving home for very long, without taking the children, was an essential rule. Attending church religiously, hoping faith would instill some recompense in my husband, was another rule. Noting he was at times a gentle giant. This was a highly intelligent yet solemnly unproductive man outside of the United States military. Ambition was down-played in his family growing up, so he just never developed it. Less is more was his adage. He too was abused as a child and only knew abuse as discipline.

I left him when the children were eight (8), five (5), four (4), three (3) and five (5) months old. I made it past twenty-five (25), I was twenty-seven (27) when I left him. I worked from home and managed to hide $20.00 unbeknownst to him. I'd gotten a Dodge Dart Swinger from his Gunny Sergeant and wife . . . so at 11PM at night, I loaded my babies into the car along with their five pillows and blankets and left him and our home on Camp Pendleton USMC base.

Afterward, the military command had him move into barracks and asked me to move the children back into base housing until the separation was in place. The housing was being renovated and we were the last family in the units. Communications were knocked out, and at night I'd have to remain awake all night because he would try to break in and there was no way to call anyone. Cell phones were science fiction at the time.

Finally, I managed to move to a duplex in a nearby town, to attend college and to work two jobs while receiving child support sporadically. Backpacking babies to school and daycare two miles each way, before catching a bus to college was eventful. The Dodge Dart Swinger needing an oil change and brakes, the ex-offered to repair and being naive I said okay. He took the steering mechanism out, he repaired the brakes so they went out randomly, and the door jams would suddenly fly open when we turned a corner. So . . . hoofing it became a learning experience and, of course, no more ex-husband car repairs.

Love.Life.memories..............................

Needless to say – ours was not a trellised experience.

"white walled haripines" reveals the reality of marital achievement when unequally yoked.

STOP RAPE NOW

NO MEANS NO

Canvassed Navel and He Said Not

To Pick Lint Hairs

city lights
housing street
hums

portabello crops
poured on checkered cloths

meadows
lands
seaports

he stood.

naked suited
with angulations.

Canvassed Naval and He Said Not Back Story

In studying Ferlinghetti and others with whom I've held a fascination over quadrants of time – I developed an image of good. It is transcendent.

Love.Life.memories...........................

"canvassed naval and he said not to pick lint hairs," shares an image of a man and a woman, their lifetime of eventful exchanges and understandings with a presumption Ferlinghetti wasn't abusive.

Strength. Compassion. Education. A world free of domestic violence

Domestic Violence Awareness

Canvassed Navel and He Said Not To Pick Lint Hairs Reviews

You had me at the fantastic title . . . Your words weave an invitation to explore and walk in the shoes of those your poetry renders immortal . . . Beautiful work indeed my friend.

Peace,
Bill :-)

succinct and slightly off.center . . . a swiftly tilting world in which everything black mirrors itself . . .

i really adore your voice.

i may have to 'bookmark' you . . .

indeed~ness

Blue Soplain

Splendor and wonder so simply woven to present a life like a portrait, well done . . .

Be always safe,
Karen Palumbo

Beautiful Poetic verses,

Well Penned.

Love & Peace be with you always.
William

Dramatic in its presentation, and the picture adds so much to this one as the words and images flow as one.

Fee

Hello Donna,

I see why this poetic expression is a favorite of yours & the perfect pic to showcase your writing!

Love It!!

Embrasse'
Vickie

Mushrooms and food for thought . . . poetry travels from afar here Donna . . . puts me in the frame of an old "talkie" in b & w cinema, W.C. Fields / Mae West screening . . . be well . . .

Warmly,
Sage

Beautiful write indeed my friend, so much said within few lines. Enjoyed!

Blessings,
Joyce B.

Oh, I love this, so few words and an entire story unravels. My favorite part is the last line. Perfect!

Janet xoxoxo

Marci's Mouse

gazing at potteries,
marred earthen clays,
polished glasses and crystal;
cobwebs find their way.

a mouse sinters by,
                we see him.

we sit. elbows rest hard,
on the wood tiled table,
an off balanced leg resides
atop a neatly folded menu~

placed by marci.
                    a repair is needed.

the dancing sun
in vibrant revelry
shoots orange translucent beams;
that pierce glass windows.

flickers of light arrive,
we bounce reflections
over the tiles,
a forth and back off buttery knives.

but menus grow weary,
                    as this table shakes.

we imagined light sabers
where pain is not allowed.
the sun fades; it is an overstated
curtain call to a starlit darkness.

we didn't believe in mousetraps.
                    mice chide that fact.

Marci's Mouse Back Story

Early in life, my memories recall assortments of personalities at kitchen tables always busy in conversation over beverages. Whether tea, coffee, juice or soft drinks, there was never the romanticism of a naturally played acoustic guitar, accordion or tambourine but the melody of humanity revealed a centrist's theme . . . unilateral interest without end game ideations.

As time progressed, conversations shortened. Human beings no longer introduced themselves through the back door as they entered and kicked off shoes. The romance of consciousness from young and old alike dwindled in this incessant march toward future progress. Our kitchen table moved to a formal dining area and discussions featured timing with an understated regulatory oversight.

Later, the only culprit of communication who seemed a truest . . . was the mouse . . . who peered up at us in the kitchen waving nonconformity's flag. The mouse watched us as we left him behind in our movement toward formal dining. And, being a mouse, he continued to saunter by waving his hat at our unrecognized disparities. The hat changed to include shades, a feather and buttons for mouse events. Then tambourines and flutes entered. Later, accordions. The last mouse held up his acoustic guitar, glared at me and puffed on a Cuban cigar while drinking French sauvignon. Supported by a leftover English cottage design tiling . . . this mouse sat atop a block of wood with old thread spools made into makeshift chairs. A collection of his micey folk strolled in our back door, wearing top hats, shawls, costume jewelry and even togas. They wrangled in mouse fashion wielding tall tales, rumors and futurist ideals at one another. It was a sight to see, and I recognized no one else saw them except Marci who winked at me in a secretive exchange.

We'd intended to share our love at a formally adorned dining room with menus but all we'd achieved was the acquisition of "one" copy of "one" menu, which we sat atop the wood tile table for viewing as an achievement – we almost dined "there." Eventually, embracing our compendium of personalities atop the wood tile table a waffling would begin. As the sun entered our kitchen the musky aromas lifted to mystic levels, and rays of light bit at them dissipating into an early morning fog; Marci folded the would-be visionary formal eatery bill of fare and placed it under a leg to steady our consumptions.

Love.Life.memories..................................

    This work speaks about progress and its lack of progression. As well as the act of engagement while often being disengaged. It seeks to restore a naturalist's sense of well-being and achievement. Much about the recoveree and self-contentment. The act of knowing.

Marci's Mouse Reviews

Well, done!

m.j. hollingshead

Sweet, (mice are cool). Sweet pictures come to mind with this, real pretty.

Rose Lova

I have missed you. You haven't lost your touch to delight with wonder! Well, done!

(((HJGS))) and love, Karla.

Well, presented. Cute story.

Best wishes,
Joyce Devenish

Very beautifully presented unique poem Donna! Good to read you again!

Love,
Eileen T. Waldron

Live and let live in a beautiful setting that enhances your poem.

George Carroll

Vivid images embellish this setting where man and mice share an eviron where the mice seem to have the upper paw . . .

jude forese

This took this reader on a verse-to-verse image of beautiful colors and mice that creep about in the darkness, not having to worry about being trapped. Your thought processes keep the voice flowing perfectly. I like this writing.

Barbara Smith

As Fee said, what more could a mouse ask for? Beautiful poem and beautifully styled.

Ted L. Glines

Beautiful layout and format combined with a winning combination of topic with wonderful word play, no mice could ask for more . . .

Felix Perry

Nice . . . a very nice work of thoughts within poetry . . .

Enjoyed....Art Sun...

A beautiful appreciation of nature in all its rustic splendor.

Mr. Larry Lounsbury

Crafted so well, this poem and the art presentation with poem on it . . . Nice JOB. I enjoyed the read.

Jocelyn M.

Satisfaction's Lament

◇◇◇◇◇◇

we've masticated these bones
to the point they resemble #2 pencils
warped like the souls who wield them.
flesh in supposition has lost its flair,
providing no new amplifications.

saffron tea leaves shaken in broken cups,
used to carry the images of future lore.
they just settle now as unscathed queries.
spirits hear the discontentment,
providing no new redress to poignancy.

◇◇◇◇◇◇

Satisfaction's Lament Back Story

At times, people seem so preoccupied with storytelling they lose one another. And, at other times, it has seemed to me conversation and storytelling, is reminiscent of pencils in school at test taking season. We've all seen those pencils so chewed on they are covered in teeth prints. While never actually viewing the culprit of a pencil death scene, I've always imagined hypertensive and anxiety ridden pencil gnawers to be likened to corn on the cob contestants at an eating contest.

Again, sexuality and its lack of spirit results in the flesh in supplication losing its flair but also in masticating our stories to agonizing proportions that nothing sheds new light on our conversations.

The old lore of tea readings and taking time to drink a heavy cup of conversation over the formality of décorated tables with attire mating to an occasion gave us satisfaction without the story. The former acts of pretense and procedural, as treatises for our tall tales in and of themselves, gave a certain pleasure through formality – the time share was richer and the message was as well.

Instead, we live in an era where there is no fermentation or even processing in the art of communication. It is a lamentation we share instead and the satisfaction derived in sharing noteworthy vignettes or the obscurities of mind, no longer have poignancy. And even the beings beyond the veil of our realm of consciousness hear our reprieve of being so riddled with innocuous information shed without fanfare, without recourse, without consideration ~ they too turn to yawn and walk away.

love.life.memories.............................

This is a story about stories and their effect on relationships. At times, the old rituals of dress, preparation, appointments, and then sharing of "news" that gave us time to best appropriate our data seem a lost art form, which deserves reawakening.

Today, we tend to spew at one another. There is so much we share — we have nothing left to divulge. And reality television also exacerbates the spewing by taking a place as one of "satisfaction's lamentations."

The Passion Is Rising Its Taking Its Own Path

films on house wares bother her
at the kitchen table.
her eggs and bacon are reminiscent of still life.

there's a cobweb in the corner.
she notices it when she takes her seat,
a mental note is planted.
the ladder and dust mop are too distant now.

the china tea cup houses saffron lemon
with cracks and fissures she loves.
it provides a history.
all good moments deserve lasting images.

thoughts shift to the gardener
with chiseled flesh, he resembles
an early dutch painting.
she thinks of their last conversation,

he was holding a rhododendron
commenting on its heartiness.
lines on his eyes gave his age away,
they should talk again she thinks

her weight shifts in her chair.

The Passion Is Rising Its Taking Its Own Path Back Story

There's finally a time in a woman's life where she is aware of who she is, what she is, what she has and what she has hoped for. In that serenity, films on housewares still bother the queen in her castle. A truly gratified woman; however, no longer allows soot to control her. That crazy *need to* perpetually clean films and dust as if they were the avenues where controlling elements of life dissipate is discarded in the established woman.

Every woman has a period of life where she is either driven to madness by cleaning or driven mad by not cleaning. It is hardwired into our consciousness from birth. We are the keepers of clean or lack thereof. Wherever we rest our heads – the clean is a rite of passage and it is systemic of the greater "cleanliness of personage," which emanates from the recesses of time. And the ideation of "rest" is an empirical word. Because if we are not clean – we cannot truly rest as women.

Women reach the Inner Goddess pulpit while cooking, polishing, sewing, gardening, birthing, painting, nursing, etc. We live like a still life. Our inner Picasso parades all-around us. We see the artist in our husbands, our children, our lovers, our friends, our associates and all those we entertain, educate and love. Our passions rise. We give them away and oftertimes – the cracks, fissures, and frailties; those parts of life that need mending, dusting, and more cleansing we note on an ever-present list perpetuated from birth. The good woman's list of "to-do's," which is never a complete act final scene, finished screenplay.

Until finally, one day, we understand our power.

Love.Life.memories............................

"the passion is rising it's taking its own path" shares the reality women can choose to sit in a favorite chair and relax. Women are allowed to let dust settle. We can see a friend in the spider and her web in our corner. She builds her hopes yet another day and we once again conquer the corners of our world. In so doing — we extend a silent gratitude — the spider shares a web of private moments no one else sees. In fact, she creates private moments.

And, sometimes, the gardener just outside of view, sees the plants we need the most. He shakes them and reminds us of our still life of hearth and home is indeed alive and well in the universe.

After husbands leave and children drift away; the gardener is prepared to share our moments of cobwebs and housewares and sees them as part of the power of our silent glory.

Nosferatu's Male Lament

canines puncture flesh

with instrumental precision.

a quick rip-

a slighted tare-

as love's energy bursts open wide.

it's a course . . .

pulse quickens, as a tawdry

                                        lamentation faithfully wields

        a fixated pupil–
                a convert defiled–
                        as this feast satisfies hunger.

it's an act . . .

provocation heals no wounds

                                        viral exchanges seed depths

        a delivery–
                a release–
                        as a refreshing reawakening.

it's an era . . .

                                        . . . and there's no trail of blood

Nosferatu's Male Lament Back Story

Nosferatu, necuratu, nesuferitu and nefârtatu are commonly translated as "the unclean," "the insufferable one," or "the devil" who demonstrates the worst in male attributes. The penetration of flesh and all elements of living is Nosferatu's intent. The unclean subverts wielding provisiorary blows establishing and satisfying insufferable hunger.

Bloodlust marries primal sensibilities with the epitome of human frailties. In his unholy drive to feed and survive . . . Nosferatu is driven to irstruments, having lost his own humanity.

Love.Life.memories............................

This work was produced near Halloween and snares the intonation sexual assault is derived from — unholy acts of demonic proportions.

Courage. Respect. Compassion.

Our sorrows and wounds are healed only when we touch them with compassion.
—Buddha

Sexual Assault Awareness

Nosferatu's Male Lament Reviews

I like this, great imagery! If not for the title, I would have taken this to be about making love, though in a way it is.

JJ Johnson

Intense and enlightening write that looks at man's most primal instincts in the times of the universe that man should no longer be feeling primal.

Felix L. Perry

Gothic DOG----MA! Vampyric qualities with canine tendencies . . . sounds bestial in a good way! Position the drawbridge, I'm in the moat coming in! GRRRRRRRR . . . bite me . . .

Sage Sweetwater

A most intriguing piece, Donna.

Mr. Ed

Great pen . . .

Hugs,
Chantilly Lace

Vampires, a tale unto themselves. Good writing!

Be safe,
Karen

A great vampire tale. Loved this poem.

Larry Lounsbury

SEXUAL ASSAULT

POWER   MONEY   CONTROL

April is Sexual Assault Awareness Month. Sexual assault is a serious violent crime affecting millions of men, women, children, and their loved ones. Learn more about how and why these crimes are committed, and what to do if you or someone you know is a victim.

Tawdry Times (Adult Language)

there's a me in the you - i miss the we.

real men and women. where are they?

stuck in this nuevo reality of pretension.

sucking meat off fleshy bones of carrion,

sows and cows. lipping occasional vegies.

talks about propriety, with belches wild and farting.

flatulence once a hidden occurrence

where propriety was the norm. yet, speak the

wrong terms, all hail the war of consequence.

between jell filled faces, plumped lips, lipo

suctioned asses lean fingers drip with

cunt juices, waving Gucci bags, painting war

faces in drunken stupors. sex wags her

vital signs. as if monkey love made a real

vestibule out of the crypt called womb today.

he battles the ranges there. among the heartless.

with socks unfurled, laying like captives across

a wooden dresser. dishes stacked – stuck

remains of dead carcasses. trash overflowing.

remnants of yesterday. stench rising.

capitalist dogma stark and overstated. a past

hung out to dry on lines of conquests

shaking tits and ass while cavorting wildly. Giving

an arch, for rear entry, where towels get draped

on overly swollen cock. striking bushes hoping

for anguish - he stabs them repeatedly calling

movements affections. hand holding and kisses

remain modern acts of love. penetration and

seminal fluid exchanges of drips and drabs and

lipsticked remnants mean nothing

but vile interpretations.

a little boy was abused.

Tawdry Times Back Story

Relationships are laden with many layers today. Much like a blooming onion, we need to peel back the pretenses, which often serve as deflection devices shielding us.

The vulgarities mentioned in tawdry times were not intended to incorporate the seven deadly sins according to God; however, includes them metaphorically by chance: envy, gluttony, greed, laziness, lust, pride and wrath. These seven sins are often commonplace and descriptive of the loss of potential a man may demonstrate after being raised in abuse as a child.

Love.Life.memories............................

For the adult survivor of child abuse, sexual assault and/or domestic violence, propriety seems illusive in our encounters with others. Being more sensitized, the misnomers of propriety are translucent to survivors.

Tawdry Times Reviews

Very timely and strongly written.

Jeff Mason

The terror; the sadness; the heart shattering truth told in bold, no holds barred poetry--excellently penned nightmare. The ending takes your breath away . . .

(((HUGS))) and love, Karla. :(*tears*

Hi Donna - your writing is very strong, it makes me think, and as I have been thinking about the subject of abuse a lot recently, to find your poem here today has had quite an impact. I have been writing my way through similar subject matter and tend to keep my head down while doing so - thanks for your comment, which led me here, i feel many things reading your poem, most of all, that i would like to wish you well . . .

Nicky Goodman

Vivid, to say the least. Raises the question of how to stop it when so much pain goes unsaid.

Ronald Hull

Holy Moly . . . I am speechless . . . you took the wind right out my sail most honest and blatantly powerful offering!!

Happy Easter
Love Tinka Boukes

I am left simply wordless by the power of this writing I wish you love and peace,

Regis Auffray

My God Donna - this one must have dragged you over the coals when you wrote it. I don't know what to think about this.

Light and Wisdom,
Richard Cederberg

Yikes, I have to refrain . . .

Andy Turner

I agreed with Edward this is one powerful and shocking write but one that tells it like it is. The disgust for the treatment and the anger for the person doing this rises like a thermometer in a furnace. Very strong stuff in this one.

Fee

A truly sad piece, and a most appropriate title, Donna.

Ed

I never really had to walk away from a poem before this is the first time its power was overwhelming and I guess a little close to home.

You did a great job of expressing the feeling and also the statement of today's society.

Edward Lupinacci

You Remain!

lucidity, she dances
a lot like me
on moonlit eves
under subtle light

where clothes can
be discarded without
knowledge of the gods

you'd hoped i
would perform these
theatrics unscathed
for your potential erections

rather though
i hid the
ritualistic venues

in my dark chambers
remembering my jesus
loves you, forgive me
as i forgive you

You Remain Back Story

A healthy couple shares a certain lucidity.

Love.Life.memories.............................

This poem reveals the complexities of basic acts of love and joy after a lifetime of exposure to violence and aggression.

CONSENT is *sexy*

You Remain Reviews

Great writing, very memorable.

Duane Weide

You have an incredible way with words! Excellent writing!

Dawn Anderson

Great Poem.

Derryn Murphy

Hello Donna,

This read gave me thought to love's passions & then to betrayal, and forgiveness as you so well stated in your last stanza.

Embrasse'
Victoria's Poetry & Voices of Muse ~ Vickie

Wow Donna I am looking forward to reading more of your work, you have a wonderful way with words . . . Thank you for sharing.

Hugs,
Rose Rideout

I am mesmerized by the power of this pen - memorable lines - exquisitely penned - my new favorite of yours - saving this one to get lost in, again and again -

Karla Dorman

Someone lusted? I guess all us men and women are guilty of that, Taking action would be the wrong thing maybe? You have a neat style!

Ron (Sketchman) Axelson

Nice work . . .

Art Sun

Unspoken truths mixed with very passionate expressions, well done . . .
Karen Palumbo

Oooooo . . . very nice!

Dark Knight

Well, done!

J. Hollingshead

I love the cadence of this and the way the writer reaches out but also directs her images to the reader, I cannot speak for others but I think most males will feel this one deeply and search back to see if they are guilty of past victimization. Very nice write indeed.
Felix Perry

He Carried His Weight

- he carried his weight -

-|-

the poet - man of parables

cellblock rested

performed spoken words

truth — peace - unuttered by carrion

referred to sons / daughters

of god in a heaven

-|-

friday morning, sky murky,

tinge of grey, potential rain.

rousting giants — jarred him

the poet - he stood.

a not so well respite

left him weary, aching.

-|-

sleepy man eyes with

no opportunity to

brush teeth, comb hair.

through a doorway shoved

awareness | acceptance

torture she is the brutality of love.

-|-

crossing dry ground sandy footed.

prodded and demeaned.

leather strained flesh struck.

bones that lay barely hidden

passerby euphemisms spat as

the poet spoke of laments,

-|-

incongruence, internal messages

truths - reflections

shone from rivers, ponds, or

shiny objects compiled riches

realizations — knowledge - undesirables

drugged with destiny

-|-

carried his weight

over tormented body

through village paths

hills and plateaus - aiding

that burial called death

pierced and watching

-|-

vain repetitions - impalements,

salty quenches of thirst

a poets glance - in wretched pain.

expressions of love, siblings tender.

immortals glances — he uttered

the final physical quatrain.

-|-

it is done.

"Mental Pain is LESS DRAMATIC THAN PHYSICAL PAIN, but it is more common and also more hard to bear."

C.S. Lewis

He Carried His Weight- Back Story

Torture she is the brutality of love.

How did Jesus's last day prevail? When he awoke to take his final journey toward physical death, rebirth and ascension — what was his morning ritual like?

Did the Christ have weary sleep? Did he sleep? Was his face caked with the remnants of sleep? Did he have an opportunity to get a drink and run to the bathroom?

The day-to-day we engage in a routine manner our Lord could not even entertain in death.

Love.Life.memories.............................

It crossed my mind we often think of the lashes and the rebirth and ascension of Christ to heaven - but what of his last day on earth in physical form pre-crucifixion?

This was an attempt to capture a last day of a condemned man incorporating his humanistic and Godlike qualities.

Support Advocate Cure
Hope Inspire Faith
Awareness
Research
Determination
Mental Health Awareness

He Carried His Weight Reviews

A lovely write . . . I am a Christian too and I do prison ministry.

Thanks,
JMD

Donna, When I am under attack and life seems hard to bear, I see those images and think who am I to complain they haven't crucified me yet. Christ along with being my savior is the man I most admire of those who have lived on this earth. He carried the weight of us all.

Larry Matthews

Good write.

Blessings,
Luke

Outstanding write Donna!! Thanks for sharing!!

Love Tinka

Exceptional write Donna, thank you for sharing with us. Wishing you and yours a blessed Easter, hope the bunny is good to you too.

Hugs,
Rose

Your Hearts Passion Was Poured Into Your Words For This Poetic Express!

Your Poem For Christ Is Spoken From Him Through You As Your Depiction Was With Excellence & Ease Of Your Verses Speaking! Excellent Poetry Donna!

Embraced~Embrasse'
B essing Too :)
Vickie

Quite the contrary, you have done him justice through your heart wrenching words of sincerity. Jesus suffered like no other before or after. Wishing you and your family a most spiritual Easter . . .

Karen

Beautiful writing of our Savior's last hours on earth. I especially liked the third stanza, because it makes Him seem that much more real.

Dawn Anderson

EXCELLENT poetry of the last hours of Jesus.

Blessings,
~Linda Hill

A poem depicting what might have gone through Christ's" mind that Good Friday morning. Inspiring and awe filled.

George

Our Lord? You are Christian Donna? I never would have guessed.

Jesus a Poet? The God of the universe in flesh relegated to being a poet? I don't know Donna. An interesting postulation though.

I do believe that He was one given to speaking in Holy Spirit inspired riddles (parables) to His own; those who embraced Him as the Christ, the son of the Living God. And the Holy Spirit was He who allowed the listener to understand the deeper spiritual truths of what the average pagan earth-dweller, and phylactery bound Jew never could.

Doing justice to this concept (as you mentioned in your prologue) is certainly relative. In order for one to understand your heart and intentions they would have to have their understanding opened up by the Holy Spirit. This write effectively changed my opinion of you.

Richard Cederberg

Prosthetic Amusement

**bereft through living
she examined her
post-humus musings
determined some of them
to shallow
ineffective and less than
stellar glimpses of times**

but . . . she trekked onward
toward the pillars of note
taking and speculative
jottings to perhaps stimulate
emotive panderings or chagrin
of those with whom took their
time to ponder her grey matters.

she misses him like a limb
or the prosthetic replacement
she misplaced yet another time.
no she misses him like she
misses herself the she that only
shines in his presence–the she
that was top shelved early in life
for the oh so safe keeping.

he knows that. so she returned home.
for good measure and the sake of hope.

Prosthetic Amusement Back Story

Hearts are to some mere morsels, much like liver enveloped in onion driven rains.

Some hearts become torrents . . .

But to others they resemble delicate flagships to be housed in glass bottles and then placed intricately on mantels for a lifetime of viewing . . .

Yet to others, the heart is like the marshmallow goodness as consumptively delicious s'mores of living.

It is my hope we all obtain a dose of flagship intricacy coupled with the passion of marshmallow goodness.

It is my prayer.

Love.Life.memories...........................

This poem was written after romance and an unachievable amity due to circumstances beyond love. This work speaks to the knowledge of se f and union as life's best ritual for coupling when the semantics of living create an unattainable outcome. Both parties may complement one another in the best manner of their lifetime and this does not always result in the possibility of unification in the day-to-day logistics of life. In these instances, the heart, the soul, the mind, the memory, the spirit can be a prosthetic amusement as jesters in our own courts.

They say, "Knowing is half the battle."

For the survivor of child abuse or sexual assault the "top shelved for the *oh so safe keeping*" is extremely commonplace. What better way to mitigate the world, after being robbed of the capability to experience the innocence of a first or second or real love and to have the ability to build faith and trust in another human being permanently torn asunder? It is not unusual for the survivor of abuse, assault or violence to let go of the hope of a tryst in exchange for the comfort of the lack of risk – even if the soul understands there is no risk – the trauma controls the survivor. While knowing is one-half the battle — it may still be the loosing half.

And then . . . there is always hope.

FREE
FROM
THE THREAT
OF
FEAR
AND VIOLENCE

Prosthetic Amusement Reviews

WOW, I bow to your pen and am honored to share space in this den with real poets. In gratitude forever for caring to share. You are truly a phenomenal woman. (Reference is to your bio. 5 children)

M. Bennett Hooper

When it comes to love...whether in its infancy stage, its passionate 'middle' or the pains culminating in its demise . . . one thing is for certain. There is always "hope."

Well written,
Anna Marie Fritz (Reader)

What better reason . . .life is like a rollercoaster ride!!

Love Tinka

It sometimes makes me cringe to think what we have come to accept at times, for the sake of others, and for hope of something better, which is like a toss of the dice...Excellent poem Donna!

Eileen T. Waldron

Ah, for the sake of hope, what better reason? How well you have orchestrated this beauty . . .

Be always safe,
Karen

Oh, I Can Feel The Yearning Of Missing This Type Of Loss. This is a very well worded poetic express my friend :)

Embrasse'
Vickie

How often we come to depend on the love in our life as we do our hands, feet etc. to pull us through the life we are so accustomed to. Thank you for sharing your words with us Donna.

NewfieHugs,
Rose Rideout

Like a jojo, oh dear, does this happen often . . . ha!

Blessings!
Jasmin Horst Seiler

Interesting and very effective with the stunning image that you have chosen. Sometimes a one-sided love or a captured trophy heart can leave that person feeling the inadequacy of not being wanted. Well, done Donna.

Mr. Felix Perry

Love does have a strangle hold that is hard to just walk away from and not know you miss it.

Mr. George Carroll

Mon dieu . . . a heavy intimate portrait of what i interpret as some self. Isolationism; and that image to convey above [vey surreal indeed; thought immediately of Dali, but stand corrected] . . . and your words illustrate that st.ringed attachment to all things intangible and esoteric that we have . . . phantom pain.ts and gentle imagined wings that hold us and keep us free simultaneously . . . this was just luminous but a tint of something akin to forlorn . . . not quite despairing, but trying to hold on or let go both . . . again . . . wow.

Ms. Soplain

It Is Not Your Place to Question Why

~it is not your place to question why~

◇◇◇◇

veins course his blood
now vintage renditions
she pricked her finger
noting the taste - bittersweet
dancing celluloids
drip to her thigh

◇◇◇◇◇

his blood courses her veins
congealing replications
he pricked her hymen
noting the religion - solemn rapture
in irreverence
remaining deep

◇◇◇◇◇◇

their course was blood
sealed for eternity
they pricked the veil
noting realisms - elucidate nature
a pact in prayer

forever combined

◇◇◇◇◇◇◇

It Is Not Your Place to Question Why Back Story

In the consummation of lust, anger, love or passion it is fairly routine for "others" to become embroiled in the discussion of "why." Interrogations arise from the general public, friends, acquaintances, family, church, and community, seemingly the universe all ask "why?"

What is the reason to become blood relatives?

It is an officious question when blood has a lasting effect on everyone who encounters it. In yesteryear, no one dared consider an act of inhibition without first testing one's blood and ensuring there was a measure of safety therein.

And blood meant generations of prodigies and was built on past-generations of labor and acquisition. To shed the veil of vintage renditions, through a seeming act of self-mutilation in allowing a hymen to be pricked requires either a blatant disregard or serious religious reflection.

The conjoining of flesh, spirit, body, personages, faith, and blood is a surreal undertaking much more than the act of penetration and release. For a young woman to know this and to still embrace her own dancing celluloids of future hopes and dreams penned in quiet pacts of prayer with a blood-bound partner is not for us to question.

Instead, the act of sexual aggression and violence, where a woman or a man are not participatory in greeting the feast of bloodletting required to stretch their combined souls beyond the veil . . . is to question why. Why the Gods believed in an eternal seal through shed and shared blood. The consequence of it all painted on our bodies in life's own warning system – the color red.

Even on its best day – the virgin loss is beautifully brutal.

And the rapist's rendition removes the beauty and only leaves the brutality. Rather than an allowance of an elucidate nature, eternity and forever . . . just the pricks remain and blood spoils.

First is purity and innocence before God.

love.life.memories...............................

This poem acknowledges the innocence of passion in its rightful form, which is pure and gruesome all at once but still better than rape.

It Is Not Your Place to Question Why Reviews

It seems a most naturalistic approach to life-juxtaposing religion with the rapturous nature of sexual intercourse. And quite brave! By the time the intensely enjoined couple gets to "a pact in prayer," the link could not be denied. Now, you must believe me when I say I like this one most. It has undertones that when fully understood, could be climatic in nature.

Appreciating your work
Dew Platt

Oh, my, Donna, you certainly grabbed my attention with this unique and sensual rendition. I've been paired in union with the same partner for over sixty years, now, so I have a gut-like feeling for your closing phrase, "forever combined."

And in your posted picture, I'm almost sure I see my own image. Oh, well, okay, maybe I've changed a little since I struck such a pose.

A wonderful write, Donna. Now I know where to go when I want originality and class. Your site is much like a plump olive soaking in vintage gin. Did I mention how much I like plump olives?

With respect and admiration,
Mr. Richard Orey

This poem blew me away. You outdid yourself!

Mr. Edwin Hurdle

A superb reminder that the Yoni was the first symbol of worship.

Mr. Roger Ochs

Wow. You have amazed me with this. I am really in awe and mesmerized.

Ms. Tabitha Carter

A profound offering!!

Love Tinka

As you say, not our place to question but I do feel a pure innocent love here, a great write Donna. Thank you for sharing.

Ms. Rose Rideout

Profound and outstanding. Peace be with you.

Mr. William Bonilla

You surely have the gift which stands out in your poem depicting love's passion in words I could never find.

Mr. George Carroll

I'm not certain if I've read you before, but as your bio states, you know how to write. A gifted poet for sure, blessings . . .

Ms. Holly Harbridge

Fine capture of one of life's deep emotional moments.

Best regards,
Mr. Leland Waldrup

Deep and intense and open to poetic interpretation. Two young lovers who cross the line of innocence into and pass the state of pure virginity that cannot be regained.

Well written and enjoyable to read.

Mr. Felix Perry

Acres of Vanilla Hardwood

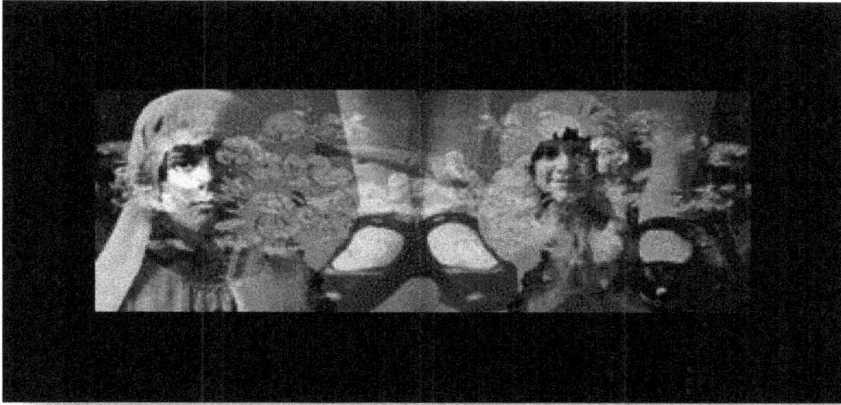

ricky-racked headboard
carries the centurions
history-conception is
that respite between sliding slats
delicately positioned
so as to not scuff vanilla hardwood.

she hates laminate surfaces.
scratching her head
remembers mother
a father - the world
where sex did not exist.

little soldier lifts unsoiled
feet towards a heaven
compares toes-singing piggies
she's demonstrating wrinkles
why they are special
love's expose' of person.

he chuckles and grabs
picture books. pointing
at plastic photos before
poking silent cheeks
mere . . . mere, smiling
with her barely lit eye.

century half past the hour

and there's life asking to live again.

Acres of Vanilla Hardwood Back Story

Love is not a quiet profession of faith. Love is noisy and boisterous and makes the floor squeak. Love bangs the headboard against the walls so the village knows it exists. Love scuffs hardwood and it doesn't mean to.

Love.Life.memories.............................

This is a celebration of love poem and I felt one poem should be shared with a positive voice because we do survive our past to glorious futures.

Life asks to live again and heals us in the many forms of love, which the village shares with us as well.

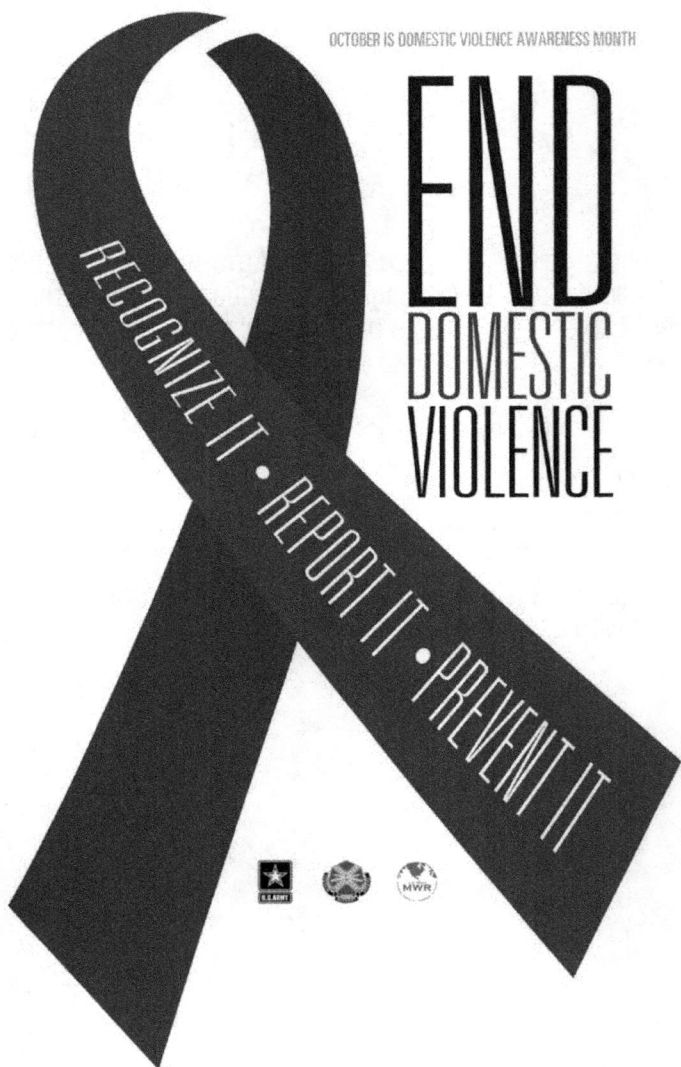

OCTOBER IS DOMESTIC VIOLENCE AWARENESS MONTH

END
DOMESTIC
VIOLENCE

RECOGNIZE IT • REPORT IT • PREVENT IT

Acres of Vanilla Hardwood Reviews

Concur with Regis, raises memories of emotion and ghosts from our own lives - could see the acres of hardwood in my life and smell Murphy (oil soap) - they say smell is the most powerful of senses - a certain odor will snap a memory like a photograph - well done!

(((HUGS))) and love,
Karla.

Your unique style shines and provokes thought and arouses emotion, Donna. Thank you.

Love and best wishes,
Mr. Auffray

Always an original voice and with unique insight; wonderfully imagined and delivered with conviction. I love this poem.

Mr. John Flanagan

Rattling bones and cold shivers, sprinkled with children's daytime laughter and nighttime tears...stunning.

Fee

Excellent poem!

Mr. Hurdle

Sheltered childhood living furniture psychology - don't mar your chastity, don't make the bed springs squeak, no blemishes, good girls don't . . . varnished interior as well as exterior . . . birthed asexual scratched vaginal with forbidden fingernails polished with the perfection of acres of vanilla hardwood . . . so many ways to interpret furniture and the psychology of lamination . . . .clear overcoat finish.

Donna . . . I do love the way you write these poems . . . very structured and unique . . . heartfelt always . . . be well.

Love,
Ms. Sage Sweetwater

Oh, this is a bit mysterious to me . . . is this lovely poem with such visual images about an elderly lady and her memories???

Hmmm, I wonder . . .

Mr. A. Pax

Prattle Flies and Dribble Bugs

hand me a bible quick
there's a dribble bug
crawling up my thigh
and he has antennas

he's posted a note on
my doorjamb-saying don't
weave or determine your
self at liberty to discuss

any self-aligned pre-
occupations with your
own humanity or concept
of some inordinate freedom.

his cage door opened
once more – he motioned
enter here, go sit down, shhhh
straighten those parlor clothes

don't prattle on about these
things that don't concern you.
sit contently and wait
my fortune to befall you

upon that last breath
after i have lived my life
you'll arise to glory
but for now – stop here.

but i have a firecracker.
i'm exploding this cage as
soon as he leaves the room
till then – i'll smile.

Prattle Flies and Dribble Bugs Back Story

Women always have prattle flies and dribble bugs crawling up toward their nether parts. Thought they appear to just be pesky little insects – it often takes a Bible pounding to reach them and send them packing.

Love.Life.memories.............................

Talking to the man who intends to rule the roost at all costs. Who ascribes a roost? And, what if she has a firecracker under her bust e?

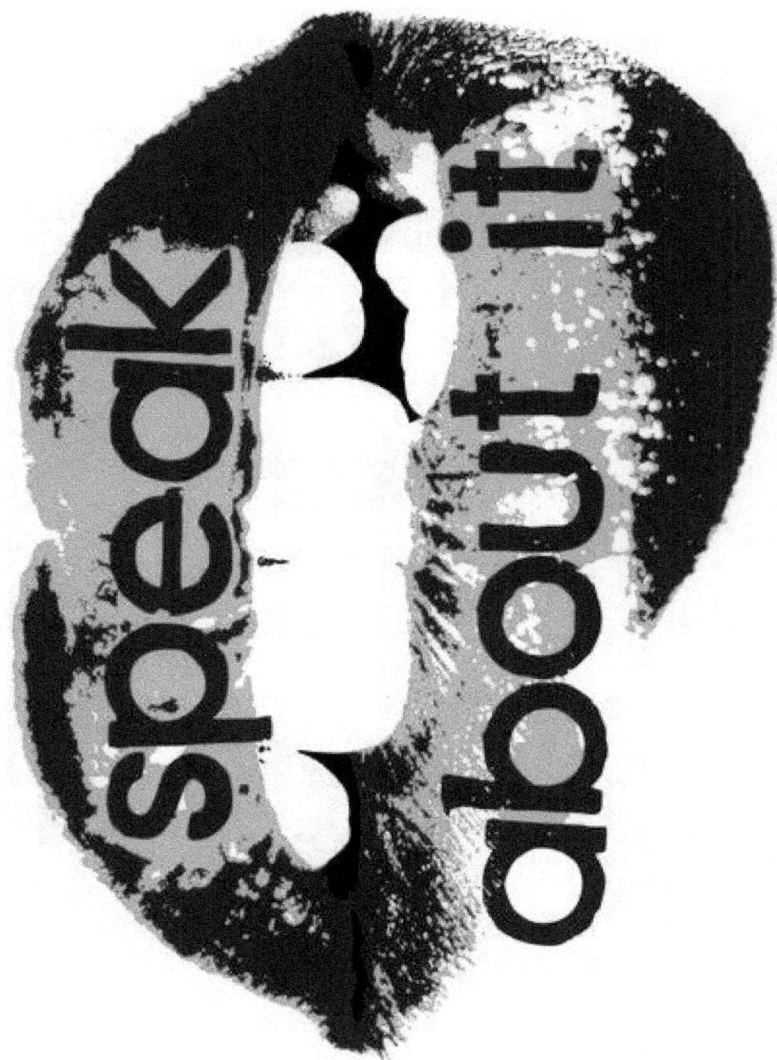

She Only Wants Pretty Poems

there was a prescription
he rendered
on whispers, in
an art of love
and war. he tallied
soap stained, languid,
with a silique.

she tried to
clarify his profundities,
to no avail.
instead-rank weariness
measured against
somber living
and the consistent
use of misuse
and discontent.

he lived in fear.

She Only Wants Pretty Poems Back Story

Communication is key to successful interactions but what of the person who is driven to manipulate in order to maintain a power position? What is worse is, "What if the person isn't aware of it?"

Many couples today share a tit-for-tat experience. Many have no idea that without some form of therapeutic intervention they are pre-disposed to using Jedi mind tricks on one another because they've lived them all their lives. And, of these people, most have parents who ensured, or they themselves suffered abuse, assault or violence in some form or another. Certainly, mental abuse is a real weapon of choice for otherwise healthy adults.

Love.Life.memories.............................

This poem addresses the hidden chambers of communication and its breakdown. Clarity is what is needed but to become clear removes the subtlety of mental manipulation and its outcome of control, which is driven by fear.

Usually, only the quiet observer sees the truth of these sort of things, which is why the villages of old had a Shaman, Priest, Chief or Wiseperson who provided clarity in a manner accepting to all parties involved in communications. At least – that's how I see it in this work.

She Only Wants Pretty Poems Reviews

Intriguing poem. Deserves a second reading and a third . . .

Ms. J'nia Fowler

A true student of human nature! Well penned.

Ms. LaBelle Rouge
Poetess of the Heart

Great write...well done!!

Love,
Ms. Boukes

Hmmmm . . . this is so real and applies to so many. It is not gender biased for I have seen it happen to both sexes and the shell that is left over is truly sad.

Mr. Felix Perry

Now this is one to read and ponder - too bad life isn't always pretty. Thank God for poets, though, who record all aspects of life, and who see the beauty amidst the ugliness of reality. I really like this one, Donna, uniquely crafted. Well, done!

(((HUGS))) and love,
Karla Dorman

A Tally of Angelic Causes

yes, in retrospect, earmarked

personal bench warrants

may be jottings in memoirs

of angels' tallied careers. heavenly

scorecard keepers render
assignment lists to check off,
and fling their successes toward
some hierarchy of celestialism

leave occasions for us - to stand
firm - as sojourners of truth,
hearing whispers that proclaim . . . *sitting*
may have befitted our moment the best.
so we sit in glazed reverence.
accolades ensue as to *"why?"*
don't we have convictions? yet,
storm barricades waving flags

in proclamation on momentous occasions
we are noted pontificators, illogical

amusement seekers. faith's ascriptions become
blind endeavors, endless questions speak
close-to-the-edge cautionary potential
of cliffed hangings. acceptance is escapist
flagrant irreverence too risky, but elective
humility is ineffecthally pompous.

sky wary gazes decry over-bearing
anticipations - lowered eyes
self-inflicted mutilations with negative
renderings. ambivalence an under
achievement, contentment lacking ideals.
rage unfortunatism of mind that seeks reproach.

in all, our guardian's tallies must result
in some unimportant discourses with god.

failed assignments, where conscripts slucclumbed.

leave the clurious to wonder . . . are

angels given work related warnings

and they reassigned other social

experiments before termination?

if so, do you think we can leary

who is next in line and then warn them?

A Tally of Angelic Causes Back Story

Survivors of abuse, assault and violence go through stages of recovery and one stage carries some name calling toward the heavens and seeks to ask, "Why didn't you intercede on my behalf?"

As a self-ascribed student of theology and angels, I tested the waters of celestial envelope pushing and angelic engagement. I arrived at the notion; angels too are weary having experienced similar activities themselves. However, they are intercessoraries for humankind.

What if we called on them to help in our hour of need or even prior to one? Can we task them to be ever-vigilant and watch over our comings and goings?

Love.Life.memories.............................

This poem addresses otherworldly entities to keep watch over us and speaks to reality no matter how we approach the subject of conviction – there's always someone who may toot a horn of opposition ascribing it a wrongful act.

This speaks to the essence of fallacies and boundaries and societally placed limitations created in the moments of our internal liberations. Each spear of destiny is met with reproach in the world of survival. As such, we need to learn how to navigate the expanse of creation and ensure the affirmations of living are extended in our direction.

And we may admonish whoever is holding the scorecards of our life histories. Action item #1: change the script . . . stop the violence.

LET'S TALK NOT FIGHT

A Tally of Angelic Causes Reviews

Thank you for this magnificent imagery and poem. God spends a lot of time in your heart and head, which is beautiful. I think when we assist one another on earth speedily we become that person or persons' angel and the wings are our heart, we have answered their prayer all orchestrated by God! Peace!!! Once again wholeheartedly thank you for this poem.

Mr. Michael Jones

Angelic causes...hmmm...interesting. I don't know any angels so I can't go there but I do know about poets called to write poems that give god all the glory and praise that he so richly deserves - I am one. I cannot speak for others but I am far from being angelic - I am a sinner living by the grace and mercy of god albeit, this is what suffers me to be one of his poets. Having been so many other things in my life, I am certainly grateful to be his instrument. This was a great write - enjoyed.

Thanks for sharing and blessings.
Ms. Joyce M. S. Bell

Wow, what a return statement, between the stunning graphic and the exceptional flow of this write...I am impressed. More please.

Hugs,
Fee

Office on Violence Against Women
Working Together to End Violence

A Perfect Orchid

i picked an orchid
an anther . . . picked

searched its crevasse
turned it upside down.

tended its filaments
to view that pistil.

wooed and venerated
a savored bouquet.

drank in all the
carpel nectar.

purified its drink . . .
positioned it delicately

within my . . . well-etched
hand blown . . . lead crystal vase

that buttercup had forgotten.

inflorescence aside,
calyx features discarded

amidst venerable petals,
it blossomed . . . atop my lace doily.

later
 . . . .it turned color

later
 . . . it crumpled

later
 . . . if fell to pieces

A Perfect Orchid Back Story

After rape — one's sexuality comes into question. Will the survivor ever successfully love the opposite sex? Is there a jaded layer of survivor reality never to be replaced with normalcy? It is statistically true, rape victims often become enamored with same sex relationships in and post-recovery.

For men, the result of male sexual assault is often a homosexual tendency. For women, they may turn against the opposing sex to become lesbian ~ this is less often the case than that of male sexual assault and resultant same sex relationships; however, all victims of sexual assault question their sexuality. There are statistics to support these realities.

Every woman I have heard states that at least once in life they suggested to themselves to become lesbian as less complicating than dealing with men in their lives. This appears to support the thought, many women are sexually abused in some way, shape or form. Conversely, men most often would not.

It would seem the level of health and wellness allotted post-assault would eliminate portions of these deviations in sexual proclivity. And deviations only meaning from the anticipated norm and not as "deviant" in and of itself.

For a number of years, I toyed with role playing in writing . . . taking on new characters, new voices, writing as a man or a woman. Writing as a lesbian or a homosexual. Writing as an emotionally solid thinker or as a broken vessel. Taking on new characters really expanded my presentation; however, I learned readers usually believe whatever a poem is centered on — it is a personal revelation — but many works I've written were composed in third person as someone else experiencing something and not my "own" personal experience at all, which I found confounding where readers presumed the sentiments must be personal experiences.

love.life.memories.............................

In "a perfect orchid" I'm writing about a woman encountering and empowering herself with another woman. The orchid being representative of the physiology of womanhood. Readers generally ascribe the intonation of a flower in their reviews, which too can be ascribed to the womanhood ~ and orchids are known for their mirror of female genitalia and this work represents this fact.

A
day
To Connect
Inspire &
Heal

A Perfect Orchid Reviews

A great inception and its ineluctable demise. How beauty or anything will come to fruition and go to dust. I love your indulgence of the whole event--almost like it only lasted a day, or even a magical glimpse of much less time passed by.

Thanks for sharing,
Darkest Angel (Reader)

One of God's most beautiful flowers!!

Love,
Ms. Tinka Boukes

These are truly such unique and beautiful of flowers . . . they are like a miracle of what God seemingly gives us without trying. Vivid capture . . . crisp and clear and with an almost sensual feel about it.

Enjoyed,
Mr. F. Perry

Donna, from such sensitive handling of the pistil wooed and venerated to the savored bouquet of the carpel nectar, I read with admiration the precision, the diction, of the poetic language that gives such life and beauty and presence to this treasured orchid. - gene.

Mr. Gene Williamson

A gracious description, Donna, of one of God's most beautiful creations.
Blessings . . .
Mr. R. Cederberg

Well crafted, Donna!

Mr. Paul Judges

I find this piece meaningfully symbolic... ...and beautiful, Donna.

Love and best wishes,
Mr. R. Auffray

. . . all beauty is ephemeral, Donna, and you handle the eternal theme with style and elegance...no mush or gush, the truth of it . . . and the detail very fine indeed.

Mr. John Flanagan

High-Centered Double Blooms

nemesistic bloodlines,

corpuscle to corpuscle,

blue ribbon thornies.

rose bush blossoms

thrive – here to there.

tiny tea hybrids,

climbing grandifloras,

gardeners' surprises.

pasteurized heirlooms,

English blends, and old

garden lore - cultivated

in hard soil vintage pots.

a few ramblers, rugosas,

sweet surrenders, and Grand

Thomas's. even veteran's honor.

ground cover, a black baccara,

germinations. an ill-formed

original double-red knockout,

removed from iridescent safety.

their well fashioned arboretum.

flourished a rogue non-

thorny. seeded. rooted.

in high-centered, double,

bloomed resonance.

the art of roses.

EQUALITY
CARING
TRUST
CARING
CONSENT
EQUALITY
RESPECT
SAFETY
CONSENT
LOVE
HEALTHY
HONESTY
HEALTHY
COMMUNICATION
RESPECT
SUPPORT
LOVE
TRUST
TRUST
COMMUNICATION
CARING
HONESTYTRUST
TRUST
COMMUNICATION
LOVE
CONSENT
COMMUNICATION
CONSENT
EQUALITY
CARING
RESPECT
SAFETYTRUST
SAFETY
LOVE
HEALTHY
COMMUNICATION
CONSENT
EQUALITYLOVE
TRUST
RESPECT
CARING
SAFETY
RESPECT
RESPECT
SAFETY
CARING
LOVE
HONESTY
SUPPORT
HEALTHY
SUPPORT
SUPPORT
TRUST
SAFETY
HEALTHY

High Centered Double Blooms Back Story

Families are like flowers. There are hearty varieties and there are haughty varieties. Fashioning the attributes of people to flowers is an innocuous way of sharing story with no harm, no foul.

Love.Life.memories..............................

"high centered double blooms," is a story of family and ancestry following a genealogical vent ascribed to one of nature's finest . . . the rose. This is meant to be a fun romp in the garden poem and a healthy way to heal.

LOVE FAITH HOPE & Mental HEALTH AWARENESS

High Centered Double Blooms Reviews

Splendid picture and poem, Donna.

Mr. Judges

. . . I am very happy to find your poem "high-centered double blooms," particularly since I have a garden and I love growing flowers.

I love flowers, not in bouquets

Alive, not cut in any ways

I care for them, give them room

In return they show me their bloom.

Love,
Ms. Emile Tubiana

A beautiful rose just as you are, Donna . . . I've seen your poetry over the years bloom into beautiful petals in literary waters, and I've seen you write about thorny issues . . . it's always a pleasure to read your intellectual work . . . I'm proud to be in your garden DQ~

Love,
Ms. Sage Sweetwater

This poem really captures the beauty of roses! They are so lovely, aren't they?

Peace, love, and light,
Amber "V" Moonstone

Gorgeous, just gorgeous, Donna!

Mr. J. Flanagan

Extro

In support of this work, it is my hope readers will join in awareness campaigns. There are three sections of the Extro, which feature Presidential Proclamations, awareness campaign overviews and information regarding how to become involved in the fight against child abuse, sexual assault and domestic violence. Not every effort to end the violence is an intense requirement – you can provide light involvement or heavy involvement – it is up to you!

As an advocate to *Stop the Violence . . . Stolen Lullabies & Secret Impasses*, is joined by the *Voices Beyond the Impasse: The Reclamation Movement* awareness campaign being released April 2015. And, as part of the platform for this title, again, each purchase counts toward an awareness campaign contribution.

Take some time to review the child abuse, sexual assault, and domestic violence Presidential Proclamations, information and participation overviews that follow this Extro. Also, if you have an educational resource, convention, program or other impending presentation in 2015 and beyond – I am happy to share a reading, interview, presentation and/or speak regarding abuse, assault and violence from a survivor's perspective.

Blue
Ribbons
for KIDS

prevent child abuse
and neglect

National Child Abuse Presidential Proclamation

NATIONAL CHILD ABUSE PREVENTION MONTH, 2014

- - - - - - -

BY THE PRESIDENT OF THE UNITED STATES OF AMERICA

A PROCLAMATION

In the United States of America, every child should have every chance in life, every chance at happiness, and every chance at success. Yet tragically, hundreds of thousands of young Americans shoulder the burden of abuse or neglect. As a Nation, we must do better. During National Child Abuse Prevention Month, we strengthen our resolve to give every young person the security, opportunity, and bright future they deserve.

We all have a role to play in preventing child abuse and neglect and in helping young victims recover. From parents and guardians to educators and community leaders, each of us can help carve out safe places for young people to build their confidence and pursue their dreams. I also encourage Americans to be aware of warning signs of child abuse and neglect, including sudden changes in behavior or school performance, untreated physical or medical issues, lack of adult supervision, and constant alertness, as though preparing for something bad to happen.

To learn more about how you can prevent child abuse, visit www.ChildWelfare.gov/Preventing.

Raising a healthy next generation is both a moral obligation and a national imperative. That is why my Administration is building awareness, strengthening responses to child abuse, and translating science and research -- what we know works for kids and families -- into practice. I also signed legislation to create the *Commission to Eliminate Child Abuse and Neglect Fatalities*, and we are providing additional resources and training to State and local governments and supporting extensive research into the causes and long-term consequences of abuse and neglect.

Our Nation thrives when we recognize that we all have a stake in each other. This month and throughout the year, let us come together -- as families, communities, and Americans -- to ensure every child can pursue their dreams in a safe and loving home.

NOW, THEREFORE, I, BARACK OBAMA, President of the United States of America, by virtue of the authority vested in me by the Constitution and the laws of the United States, do hereby proclaim April 2014 as National Child Abuse Prevention Month. I call upon all Americans to observe this month with programs and activities that help prevent child abuse and provide for children's physical, emotional, and developmental needs.

IN WITNESS WHEREOF, I have hereunto set my hand this thirty-first day of March, in the year of our Lord two thousand fourteen, and of the Independence of the United States of America the two hundred and thirty-eighth.

BARACK OBAMA

Child Abuse Awareness Campaigns

National Child Abuse Prevention Month is a time to acknowledge the importance of families and communities working together to prevent child abuse and neglect, and to promote the social and emotional well-being of children and families. During the month of April and throughout the year, communities are encouraged to share child abuse and neglect prevention awareness strategies and activities and promote prevention across the country. The theme for 2016's National Child Abuse Prevention Month is, "Building Community – Building Hope." According to Child Welfare:

This year's theme, "Building Community, Building Hope," acknowledges the tremendous power in communities to address the problem of child abuse and neglect and reflects our goal of providing a multidisciplinary forum focused on intersections of research, policy, and practice related to promoting child and family well-being and protecting children, to ensure that they grow up to achieve their full potential, free from abuse and neglect.

To make an impact on Child Abuse and Neglect everyone needs to get involved. It is okay, even GREAT! to get involved and strengthen your community. To do so, you can follow these simple guidelines:

Baby Steps

- Meet and greet your neighbors
- Go to a parent meeting at your child's school
- Participate in an activity at your local library or community center

Small Steps

- Set up a playgroup in your community at homes or local park (consider inviting people who may not have children at home, like local seniors)

- Organize a community babysitting co-op
- Volunteer at your child's school through the school's administration or the parent's organization
- Encourage local service providers to produce a directory of available services that are easy to find in the community

Big Steps

- Organize a community event (a block party, father / daughter dance, parent support group)
- Run for an office in the parent organization at your child's school
- Attend local government meetings (city council or school board meetings) and let them know how important resources are in your community. Let them know how parks, strong schools, and accessible services help to strengthen your family and other families.

In recognition of the 40th anniversary of the *Child Abuse Prevention and Treatment Act*, features significant moments in the child abuse prevention timeline for the United States[13].

1974:   Child Abuse Prevention and Treatment Act (CAPTA)
The first Federal child protection legislation, CAPTA was signed by President Nixon on January 31, 1974, and marked the beginning of a new national response to the problem of child abuse and neglect. The legislation provided Federal assistance to States for prevention, identification, and treatment programs. It also created the National Center on Child Abuse and Neglect (now known as the Office on Child Abuse and Neglect) within the Children's Bureau to serve as a Federal focal point for CAPTA activities. Today CAPTA, most recently reauthorized in 2010, continues to provide minimum standards for child maltreatment definitions and support States' prevention and intervention efforts.
1982:   First National Child Abuse Prevention Week
In 1982, Congress resolved that June 6-12 should be designated as the first National Child Abuse Prevention Week.
1983:   April proclaimed the first National Child Abuse Prevention Month
In 1982, Congress resolved that June 6–12 should be designated as the first National Child Abuse Prevention Week; the following year, President Reagan proclaimed April to be the first National Child Abuse Prevention Month, a tradition that continues to this day. The Bureau's National Center on Child Abuse and Neglect coordinated activities at the Federal level,

---

13   National Child Abuse Prevention Month for 2015. Department of Health and Human Services
      https://www.childwelfare.gov/topics/preventing/preventionmonth/about

including creation and dissemination of information and promotional materials. In 1984 for example, posters, bumper stickers, and buttons displayed the theme, "Kids—You can't beat 'em." Print, radio, and television PSAs, meanwhile, urged viewers to "Take time out. Don't take it out on your kid."

1984: Child Abuse Prevention Federal Challenge Grants Act

The Children's Bureau was an early supporter of State Children's Trust Funds. Kansas was the first State to pass such legislation in the spring of, requiring revenues from surcharges placed on marriage licenses to be used to support child abuse prevention. By 1984, the number of States with Trust Funds was up to 15. That year, Congress passed the Child Abuse Prevention Federal Challenge Grants Act (title IV of P.L. 98–473) to encourage more States to follow suit. By 1989, all but three States had passed Children's Trust Fund legislation.

1989: Blue Ribbon Campaign to Prevent Child Abuse

The blue-ribbon campaign is a memorial to children who have been affected by abuse and neglect.

1991: "We Can Make a Difference: Strategies for Combating Child Maltreatment" Conference

In the summer of, Secretary of Health and Human Services Louis W. Sullivan, MD, created an unprecedented national initiative to raise awareness about child abuse and neglect and promote coordination of prevention and treatment activities. A December 1991 meeting, "We Can Make a Difference: Strategies for Combating Child Maltreatment," encouraged participants to develop action plans that could be implemented locally. Public service announcements asking the public to "Show You Care" were released during Child Abuse Prevention Month (April) 1992.

1996: The Children's Bureau named the lead agency for the Community-Based Child Abuse Prevention (CBCAP) grants

In keeping with the Clinton Administration's emphasis on collaboration and integration among child and family-serving systems, a new grants program, Community-Based Family Resource and Support (CBFRS), was created in 1996. These grants reflected the belief that public and private child abuse prevention and treatment programs must work together toward common goals. The CBFRS program (now known as Community-Based Child Abuse Prevention or CBCAP) requires State lead agencies to establish statewide networks for family support programs, support a coordinated continuum of preventive services, and maximize funding for those services.

1996: The Office on Child Abuse and Neglect and Federal Interagency Work Group on Child Abuse and Neglect are established

The reauthorization of CAPTA abolished the National Center on Child Abuse and Neglect and created an Office on Child Abuse and Neglect (OCAN) within the Children's Bureau to coordinate the functions required under CAPTA. At the same time, a Federal Interagency Work Group on Child Abuse and Neglect (FEDIAWG) was established to replace the Inter-Agency Task Force on Child Abuse and Neglect that had been active since 1988. Today, FEDIAWG includes representatives of more than 40 Federal agencies and meets quarterly with OCAN's leadership and coordination.

2001:   13th National Conference, "Faces of Change: Embracing Diverse Cultures and Alternative Approaches"

The 13th National Conference recognized the fact that our diversity enables us to bring a multitude of approaches to bear on key issues in the field of child abuse and neglect.

2003:   Child Abuse Prevention Initiative and the 14th National Conference, "Gateways to Prevention"

The 14th National Conference recognized that prevention remains the best defense for our children. To commemorate the 20th anniversary of the first Presidential Proclamation for Child Abuse Prevention Month, OCAN launched the National Child Abuse Prevention Initiative as a yearlong effort. OCAN and its National Clearinghouse on Child Abuse and Neglect Information partnered with Prevent Child Abuse America and the child abuse prevention community to produce a variety of tools and resources to support national, State, and local public awareness activities. The same year, OCAN released its Emerging Practices in the Prevention of Child Abuse and Neglect report, the product of a 2-year effort to generate new information about effective and innovative prevention programs.

2005:   Year of the Healthy Child

There was renewed commitment to make child abuse prevention a national priority. As a result, OCAN focused on making safe children and healthy families a shared responsibility, a theme that was also incorporated into the National Conference.

2007:   OCAN developed the Resource Guide held the 16th National Conference on Child Abuse and Neglect, "Protecting Children, Promoting Healthy Families, and Preserving Communities"

This encouraged communities to join the effort to promote healthy families and work collaboratively to provide responsive child abuse prevention and family support services. At the same time, OCAN invited national organizations to be national child abuse prevention partners so the message could reach a wider audience.

2007:   three grantees funded for nurse home visitation services

The Children's Bureau funded three grantees to evaluate and implement nurse home visitation services.

2008:   CB launched cooperative agreements to increase knowledge about evidence-based home visiting programs

The Children's Bureau launched cooperative agreements to generate knowledge about the use of evidence-based home visiting programs to prevent child abuse and neglect, including obstacles and opportunities for their wider implementation.

2009:   17th National Conference, "Focusing on the Future: Strengthening Families and Communities"

The 17th National Conference theme, "Focusing on the Future: Strengthening Families and Communities" reflected the resolve to continue to protect children by addressing the root causes of child maltreatment.

2010:   Patient Protection and Affordable Care Act of 2010

This act included a provision to create the Maternal, Infant, and Early Childhood Home Visiting Program.

2011: Network for Action prevention initiative kicks off

Network for Action kicked off with a meeting in Alexandria, VA, in June. Jointly sponsored by OCAN, the U.S. Centers for Disease Control and Prevention, the FRIENDS National Resource Center, and other national prevention organizations, the Network for Action is driven by three specific goals: to create a shared vision for the future of child abuse prevention, engage in shared action, and develop and strengthen prevention networks at the State and Federal levels. A second national meeting was held in April 2012.

2012: 18th National Conference, "Celebrating the Past - Imagining the Future"

The 18th National Conference was held in conjunction with the Children's Bureau's centennial celebration year and highlighted our desire to embrace our past successes, to learn from our challenges, and to realize our dream of eliminating child abuse and neglect.

2014: 19th National Conference, "Making Meaningful Connections"

The 19th National Conference marks the 40th anniversary of the Child Abuse Prevention and Treatment Act (CAPTA, P.L. 93-247).

In review of the national timeline for the continental United States concerning Child Abuse and Neglect reform, I noted a few things:

1. First, we've only begun to work toward staving off Child Abuse. As recent as 1974, the initial Child Abuse Prevention and Treatment (CAPTA) program began. And we know Child Abuse went unnoted previous to that time.

2. Second, many of these programs I've had the horor to work on as a government (federal, state, and local) and commercial contractor; however, not by intent – my involvement has been supranatural or let's say I would determine to work with an organization and then suddenly become involved with altruistic endeavors the organization surprisingly determined I'd be good to provide responses toward.

3. Third, we have really only just begun. Thirty years is a drop in the proverbial bucket when compared to recorded history and the reality of abuse having existed for millennia.

Relating to #2 above, in fulfillment of programs from 1996 onward, one opportunity I remain especially proud of was the Department of Defense (DoD), Department of the Army, Contracting Center of Excellence (CCE), Family Morale Welfare Recreation Command, New Parent Support Program – Home Visitation (Surge) (FMWRC NPSP-HV) Program. The FMWRC NPSP-HV awarded 146 master's in social work (MSW) Licensed Professional Counselors (LPC) and nurses who held parent and/or child psychiatry minors to serve the United States Army's Family Morale Welfare Recreation Command (FMWRC) Program as Home Visitation New Parent Support Service (HV - NPSS) members.

The Department of the Army's New Parent Support Service (NPSS) was an intensive program directed at first-time mothers and/or fathers geared to optimize child development and build strong families through weekly home visitation by family support staff who were to share information on parenting skills and additional services aiding first-time and issue-ridden parents. The services were made available to first-time expectant parents or parents who had recently given birth and/or families with child abuse or domestic violence issues.

The program is on-going, while the initial award was in 2007 with a projection of five years to contract renewal or re-compete / re-award. Families were intended to graduate from the program when their child reached two years of age and after the family completed program levels, which promoted:

- Parent-child interaction;

- Bonding and attachment;

- Understanding of family life stability and self-sufficiency; and

- Knowledge and understanding of community resources.

If a child reached two years of age and these levels were not completed, home visitation was to continue until the child reached the age of three. The New Parent Support Program (NPSP) offered Army families an enhanced understanding of parent and infant attachment by increasing knowledge of child development and providing connections to the support services allowing parents to become nurturing and capable caregivers. The NPSP staff consisted of licensed social workers and registered nurses who provided in-home parenting education, support, and resource linkage. The Army Chief of Staff General George W. Casey, Jr. stated:

"As we have said before, the Army takes Soldier inpatient and outpatient care very seriously and remains firmly committed to returning our Soldiers to productive careers and lives. We have made improvements but realize there is still work to be done - including work with the complex Medical Evaluation Board and Physical Evaluation Board processes. By no means is everything 'fixed' - but we are aggressively acting on what we can fix now."

The program's tenets involved:

1. **Home Visitation**: professional staff provided supportive and caring services to military families who were pregnant, or with children through the age of three years. They provided a venue to talk about your concerns as a parent or parent-to-be, and help parents learn to cope with stress, isolation, post deployment reunions, and the everyday demands of parenthood in the privacy of the family's home.

2. **Play Morning**: designed as an interactive playgroup to assist parents in learning developmentally appropriate play techniques and to help children improve their social, cognitive, and motor skills. Structured activities included singing and dancing, story time, a craft project, and free play time.

3. **12 Things to Know in the First 20 Weeks**: these classes were important to ensure pregnancy got off to a good start! New parents learned valuable information about maintaining a healthy lifestyle including exercise, proper nutrition, rest, things to avoid during your pregnancy, and other valuable resources available to you on-post and in the surrounding community. Also, discussion was centered on what occurs during prenatal visits and what various pregnancy tests mean. Sign up was available as soon as an Army member knew there were pregnant to support early physical and emotional changes.

4. **Dads 101**: class designed by men for men! Teaching new fathers about caring for a brand new, tiny, fragile baby as the most challenging job a dad will ever have to face. Because many never get the hang of t and leave childcare issues to the mom, which was determined not to be good for Mom, marriage, or the baby. The goal of this class was to provide new dads with important skills they needed to pitch in and be the best, most effective dads they could be!

5. **Infant Care & Parenting Class**: a series of four classes designed to provide parents with an understanding of their infant's world along with basic skills necessary to care for the infant. In addition, these classes provided an opportunity for "hands-on" practices assisting parents in making informed, responsible decisions about all aspects of caring for their child during those first formative years.

Program outcomes are presented in the Assistant Chief of Staff for Installation Management Deputy Assistant Secretary of the Army (Civilian Personnel/Quality of Life) for Office of the Deputy Under Secretary of Defense for Military Community and family Policy, Domestic Violence and Child Abuse Fatality Review (04 Oct 2010) the following statistics are extended:

- Fifteen (100%) of the 15 child fatalities were children under the age of four. The youngest children are at the greatest risk. This statistic is consistent with the latest national report from the US Department of Health and Human Services (HHS) in 2003, which indicates that more than three-quarters (78.8%) of children who were killed as a result of abuse were younger than four years of age (HHS Child Maltreatment 2003, Chapter 4, Figure 4-1, Percentage of Child Fatalities by age 2003).

- During the FY96-FY00 timeframe, Army rates of substantiated child abuse have steadily declined from 7.1% to 5%. During the FY01-FY04 timeframe, the rates increased from 5.2% to 6.2%. During the FY05-FY09 timeframe, the rates decreased from 5.3% to 5.2%. These rates are half of the rates for substantiated child abuse within the US civilian population (12.4%) based upon the latest statistics compiled by HHS.

- Twelve (55%) of the 22 domestic violence fatalities occurred within six months of deployment/re-deployment.

- Thirteen (56%) of the 22 domestic violence cases contained allegations of infidelity.

Recommendations: to facilitate early and effective intervention in domestic violence and child abuse cases, the FRB recommends three new policy changes for the DoD and 12 new DA policy changes. In addition, the FRB reiterated 6 previous recommendations for DoD and 2 previous recommendations for the DA.

Status of Previous Recommendations: the FRB recognizes it has a responsibility to report actions taken to date to implement prior year recommendations:

- In FY08, the Army continued to revise its guidelines in an attempt to adopt more thorough standards for death investigations. Specifically, in an attempt to collect all pertinent data for Family-related deaths, the Army began to revise its guidance to law enforcement in regard to law enforcement's joint investigations concerning Family-related deaths.

- The Army incorporated Family Advocacy Program (FAP) interventions needed when the unit is not providing the appropriate level of safety for victims of child abuse or domestic violence, the Health Insurance Portability and Accountability Act (HIPPA), and the fatality review process into the Family Advocacy Staff Training (FAST) course taught at the Army Medical Center and School (AMEDDC&S).

- The Army will continue to provide current AMEDD policy regarding Shaken Baby Avoidance at the medical treatment facilities by renewing the Shaken Baby Avoidance Policy for an additional two-year period. The policy requires a briefing for both parents prior to the newborn's release from the hospital and highlights strategies for soothing a crying baby. The Army has also published guidance drawing medical provider attention to the co-occurrence of child abuse, spouse abuse, and substance abuse issues. These co-occurrence issues have been incorporated into the FAST and Drug and Alcohol courses taught at the AMEDDC&S.

- The Army continues to stress the critical nature of early intervention and has revised the fatality review data sheet to capture New Parent Support Program-Home Visitation (NPSP-HV) involvement with Families with children less than three years of age. It has added a NFSP-HV and an EFMP representative as a consultant member on the FRB and ensured that the NPSP-HVs received training on motivational interviewing techniques for resistant clients.

- In FY08, the DA required Army garrisons to implement three prior recommendations and to report to the DA concerning their progress in implementing these recommendations. As of 1 June 2010, the implementation rates for these recommendations average 93% across all Army installations. The recommendations were designed to strengthen installation FRC member training, increase commander and key helping agency awareness of the fatality review process, increase membership numbers, and expand outreach efforts to reach Families with special needs children off post.

This is only a partial report of the entire *DoD Army Fatality Review Report for FY2010.* This demonstrates the reality that the FMWRC NPSP-HV Program was a true need for the US Army and all services – as it was incorporated among all military disciplines. When this opportunity was presented for competitive bid through HRSolutions IDIQ, I designed the End-to-End (E2) solution for my Client who had suggested a no-bid not understanding fulfillment involved nearly 200 personnel comprised of psychologists and psychiatrists and additional mental health practitioner. I convinced them to move forward with the bid, which was awarded. The solution I designed answered poor parenting and domestic relations requirements; however, my Client never really understood the solution, which as a survivor initiated progressive fulfillment. Instead, as they worked to fulfill the opportunity, in hearing the talent managers interviewing the intended personnel to staff the solution, I shared the whole emphasis of the program was being thwarted through misunderstanding of the positivity of the program intent rather than the focus on the parents as inherently ignorant. I was disappointed to see quid pro quo that results in padded files, wrongful family law practices and suffered both parents and children in 2007 and I can see (living in the communities of post-award fulfillment) it transversed to a misappropriated fulfillment practice even today.

Truly we need to re-evaluate our mindsets regarding Child Abuse and Domestic Violence and begin identifying the pink elephants in our living rooms while recognizing change comes from teaching respect and lifting self-esteem. People with self-respect and self-esteem are less likely to abuse one another.

April is **Child Abuse Prevention Month**

PROTECTING CHILDREN –IS– EVERYONE'S JOB

Sexual Assault Presidential Proclamation

NATIONAL SEXUAL ASSAULT AWARENESS AND PREVENTION MONTH, 2014

BY THE PRESIDENT OF THE UNITED STATES OF AMERICA

A PROCLAMATION

Every April, our Nation comes together to renew our stand against a crime that affronts our basic decency and humanity. Sexual assault threatens every community in America, and we all have a role to play in protecting those we love most -- our mothers and fathers, our husbands and wives, our daughters and sons. During National Sexual Assault Awareness and Prevention Month, we recommit to ending the outrage of sexual assault, giving survivors the support they need to heal, and building a culture that never tolerates sexual violence.

Thanks to dedicated activists and courageous survivors, we have made strides in reducing stigma, opened new shelters across our country, and given countless Americans a new sense of hope. A driving force behind much of this progress was the landmark Violence Against Women Act. Last year, I was proud to sign legislation that reauthorized and strengthened this law while also extending protections for underserved communities.

We have come a long way, but sexual violence remains an all-too-common tragedy. Today, an estimated one in five women is sexually assaulted in college. This is unacceptable. Because college should be a place where everyone can safely and confidently pursue their talents, I

launched the White House Task Force to Protect Students from Sexual Assault. And because our Nation's backlog of rape kits means offenders may be free to strike again, I have proposed funding for coordinated community teams to address this problem. My Administration is working to stop sexual assaults wherever they occur, in both the civilian community and the Armed Forces. Together, we will continue to strengthen the criminal justice system, develop trauma-informed services, reach out to survivors, and focus aggressively on prevention.

Sexual assault is more than just a crime against individuals. When a young boy or girl withdraws because they are questioning their self-worth after an assault that deprives us of their full potential. When a parent struggles to hold a job in the wake of a traumatic attack, the whole family suffers. And when a student drops out of school or a service member leaves the military because they were sexually assaulted, that is a loss for our entire Nation.

This month, let us recognize that we all have a stake in preventing sexual assault, and we all have the power to make a difference. Together, let us stand for dignity and respect, strengthen the fabric of our communities, and build a safer, more just world.

NOW, THEREFORE, I, BARACK OBAMA, President of the United States of America, by virtue of the authority vested in me by the Constitution and the laws of the United States, do hereby proclaim April 2014 as National Sexual Assault Awareness and Prevention Month. I urge all Americans to support survivors of sexual assault and work together to prevent these crimes in their communities.

IN WITNESS WHEREOF, I have hereunto set my hand this thirty-first day of March, in the year of our Lord two thousand fourteen, and of the Independence of the United States of America the two hundred and thirty-eighth.

BARACK OBAMA

Sexual Assault Awareness Campaigns

Sexual Assault Awareness Month (SAAM) is also held in the month of April each year. SAAM is geared to raise awareness about sexual assault and to educate communities and individuals on how to prevent sexual violence.

During April, government (federal, state, local) and commercial (community based) entities plan events to highlight sexual violence and human rights, public health and social justice that it is. Prevention efforts are shared and reinforced in April each year with the intent for 365/24/7 vigilance to aid in the fight against sexual assault.

The theme, slogan, resources and materials for the national SAAM campaign are coordinated by the National Sexual Violence Resource Center each year with assistance from anti-sexual assault organizations throughout the United States.

Sexual Assault Statistics in the United States

Sexual Violence in the U.S.

One in five women and one in 71 men will be raped at some point in their lives (a) 46.4% lesbians, 74.9% bisexual women and 43.3% heterosexual women reported sexual violence other than rape during their lifetimes, while 40.2% gay men, 47.4% bisexual men and 20.8% heterosexual men reported sexual violence other than rape during their lifetimes.

- Nearly one in 10 women has been raped by an intimate partner in her lifetime, including completed forced penetration, attempted forced penetration or alcohol / drug-facilitated completed penetration.

- Approximately one in 45 men has been made to penetrate an intimate partner during his lifetime.

- 91% of the victims of rape and sexual assault are female, and 9% are male

- In eight out of 10 cases of rape, the victim knew the person who sexually assaulted them

- 8% of rapes occur while the victim is at work

Cost and Impact

- Each rape costs approximately $151,423

- Annually, rape costs the U.S. more than any other crime ($127 billion), followed by assault ($93 billion), murder ($71 billion), and drunk driving ($61 billion)

- 81% of women and 35% of men report significant short-term or long-term impacts such as Post-Traumatic Stress Disorder (PTSD)

- Health care is 16% higher for women who were sexually abused as children

Child Sexual Abuse

- One in four girls and one in six boys will be sexually abused before they turn 18 years old

- 34% of people who sexually abuse a child are family members

- 12.3% of women were age 10 or younger at the time of their first rape/victimization, and 30% of women were between the ages of 11 and 17

- 27.8% of men were age 10 or younger at the time of their first rape/victimization

- More than one-third of women who report being raped before age 18 also experience rape as an adult

- 96% of people who sexually abuse children are male, and 76.8% of people who sexually abuse children are adults (n)

- 325,000 children are at risk of becoming victims of commercial child sexual exploitation each year

- The average age at which girls first become victims of prostitution is 12 to 14 years old, and the average age for boys is 11 to 13 years old

Campus Sexual Assault

- One in 5 women and one in 16 men are sexually assaulted while in college

- More than 90% of sexual assault victims on college campuses do not report the assault

- 63.3% of men at one university who self-reported acts qualifying as rape or attempted rape admitted to committing repeat rapes

Crime Reports

- Rape is the most under-reported crime; 63% of sexual assaults are not reported to police

- Only 12% of child sexual abuse is reported to the authorities

A History of Sexual Assault Awareness

1960s - 1970s: The field of sexual assault prevention emerges.

1975: Susan Brownmiller's Against Our Will addresses the issue of rape. Public awareness begins.

1975: Congress passes the Rape Control Act.

1970s - 1980s: Sexual violence survivors speak out and share their stories.

1984: Ms. Magazine releases the results of their Campus Sexual Assault project.

1980s: Programs to prevent child abuse and child sexual abuse emerge.

1980s: Laws are passed to prevent sexual violence.

1980s: Federal dollars are put toward sexual violence prevention efforts.

1980s - 1990s: Survivors begin to seek services.

1990s: The "era of accountability" leads to exploring how effective programs and services are.

2001: The first Sexual Assault Awareness Month is observed nationally.

2009: President Obama proclaims April as Sexual Assault Awareness Month.

Sources:

History of Sexual Assault Awareness and Prevention Efforts | ccasa.org | nsvrc.org | whitehouse.gov |

Domestic Violence Presidential Proclamation

NATIONAL DOMESTIC VIOLENCE
AWARENESS MONTH, 2014

- - - - - - -

BY THE PRESIDENT OF THE UNITED STATES OF AMERICA
A PROCLAMATION

Domestic violence affects every American. It harms our communities, weakdddens the foundation of our Nation, and hurts those we love most. It is an affront to our basic decency and humanity, and it must end. During National Domestic Violence Awareness Month, we acknowledge the progress made in reducing these shameful crimes, embrace the basic human right to be free from violence and abuse, and recognize that more work remains until every individual is able to live free from fear.

Last month, our Nation marked the 20th anniversary of the Violence Against Women Act (VAWA). Before this historic law, domestic violence was seen by many as a lesser offense, and women in danger often had nowhere to go. But VAWA marked a turning point, and it slowly transformed the way people think about domestic abuse. Today, as 1 out of every 10 teenagers are physically hurt on purpose by someone they are dating, we seek to change our culture and reject the quiet tolerance of what is fundamentally unacceptable once again profoundly. That is why Vice President Joe Biden launched the 1is2many initiative to engage educators, parents, and students while raising awareness about dating violence and the role we all have to play in stopping it. And it is why the White House Task Force to Protect Students from Sexual Assault and the newly launched "It's On Us" campaign will address the intersection of sexual assault and dating violence on college campuses.

Since VAWA's passage, domestic violence has dropped by almost two-thirds, but despite these strides, there is more to do. Nearly two out of three Americans 15 years of age or older know a victim of domestic violence or sexual assault, and domestic violence homicides claim the lives of three women every day. When women and children are deprived of a loving home, legal protections, or financial independence because they fear for their safety, our Nation is denied its full potential.

My Administration is committed to reaching a future free of domestic violence. We are building public-private partnerships to directly address domestic violence in our neighborhoods and workplaces, and we are helping communities use evidence-based screening programs to prevent domestic violence homicides. At the same time, the Federal Government is leading by example, developing policies to ensure domestic violence is addressed in the Federal workforce. New protections under the Affordable Care Act provide more women with access to free screenings and counseling for domestic violence. And when I proudly reauthorized VAWA last year, we expanded housing assistance; added critical protections for lesbian, gay, bisexual, and transgender Americans; and empowered tribal governments to protect Native American women from domestic violence in Indian Country.

Our Nation's success can be judged by how we treat women and girls, and we must all work together to end domestic violence. As we honor the advocates and victim service providers who offer support during the darkest moments of someone's life, I encourage survivors and their loved ones who are seeking assistance to reach out by calling the National Domestic Violence Hotline at 1-800-799-SAFE FREE or visit www.TheHotline.org.

This month, we recognize the survivors and victims of abuse whose courage inspires us all. We recommit to offering a helping hand to those most in need, and we remind them that they are not alone.

NOW, THEREFORE, I, BARACK OBAMA, President of the United States of America, by virtue of the authority vested in me by the Constitution and the laws of the United States, do hereby proclaim October 2014 as National Domestic Violence Awareness Month. I call on all Americans to speak out against domestic violence and support local efforts to assist victims of these crimes in finding the help and healing they need.

IN WITNESS WHEREOF, I have hereunto set my hand this thirtieth day of September, in the year of our Lord two thousand fourteen, and of the Independence of the United States of America the two hundred and thirty-ninth.

BARACK OBAMA

Domestic Violence Awareness Campaigns

Domestic violence is the willful intimidation, physical assault, battery, sexual assault, and/or other abusive behavior as part of a systematic pattern of power and control perpetrated by one intimate partner against another. It includes physical violence, sexual violence, psychological violence, and emotional abuse. The frequency and severity of domestic violence can vary dramatically; however, the one constant component of domestic violence is one partner's consistent efforts to maintain power and control over the other.

Domestic violence is an epidemic affecting individuals in every community, regardless of age, economic status, sexual orientation, gender, race, religion, or nationality. It is often accompanied by emotionally abusive and controlling behavior that is only a fraction of a systematic pattern of dominance and control. Domestic violence can result in physical injury, psychological trauma, and in severe cases, even death. The devastating physical, emotional, and psychological consequences of domestic violence can cross generations and last a lifetime.

It is not always easy to determine in the early stages of a relationship if one person will become abusive. Domestic violence intensifies over time. Abusers may often seem wonderful and perfect initially but gradually become more aggressive and controlling as the relationship continues. Abuse may begin with behaviors that may easily be dismissed or downplayed such as name-calling, threats, possessiveness, or distrust. Abusers may apologize profusely for their actions or try to convince the person they are abusing that they do these things out of love or care. However, violence and control always intensify over time with an abuser, despite the apologies. What may start out as something that was first believed to be harmless (e.g., wanting the victim to spend all their time only with them because they love them so much) escalates into extreme control and abuse (e.g., threatening to kill or hurt the victim or others if they speak to family, friends, etc.). Some examples of abusive tendencies include but are not limited to:

- Accusing the victim of cheating

- Controlling every penny spent in the household
- Controlling who the victim sees, where they go, or what they do
- Destroying the victim's property
- Dictating how the victim dresses, wears their hair, etc.
- Embarrassing or shaming the victim with put-downs
- Forcing sex with others
- Intimidating the victim with guns, knives, or other weapons
- Keeping or discouraging the victim from seeing friends or family members
- Looking at or acting in ways that scare the person they are abusing
- Pressuring or forcing the victim to use drugs or alcohol
- Pressuring the victim to have sex when they don't want to or to do things sexually they are not comfortable with
- Preventing the victim from making their own decisions
- Preventing the victim from working or attending school, harassing the victim at either, keeping their victim up all night so they perform badly at their job or in school
- Refusing to use protection when having sex or sabotaging birth control
- Showing jealousy of the victim's family and friends and time spent away
- Stalking the victim or monitoring their victim's every move (in person or also via the internet and/or other devices such as GPS tracking or the victim's phone)
- Taking the victim's money or refusing to give them money for expenses
- Telling the victim that they are a bad parent or threatening to hurt, kill, or take away their children
- Telling the victim that they can never do anything right
- Threatening to hurt or kill the victim's friends, loved ones, or pets

It is important to note that domestic violence does not always manifest as physical abuse. Emotional and psychological abuse can often be just as extreme as physical violence. Lack of physical violence does not mean the abuser is any less dangerous to the victim, nor does it mean the victim is any less trapped by the abuse.

Additionally, domestic violence does not always end when the victim escapes the abuser, tries to terminate the relationship and/or seeks help. Often, it intensifies because the abuser feels a loss of control over the victim. Abusers frequently continue to stalk, harass, threaten, and try to control the victim after the victim escapes. In fact, the victim is often in the most danger directly following the escape of the relationship or when they seek help: 1/5 of homicide victims with restraining orders are murdered within two days of obtaining the order; 1/3 are murdered within the first month.2

Unfair blame is frequently put upon the victim of abuse because of assumptions that victims choose to stay in abusive relationships (see common myths about victims of domestic violence here). The truth is, bringing an end to abuse is not a matter of the victim choosing to leave; it is a matter of the victim being able to safely escape their abuser, the abuser choosing to stop the abuse, or others (e.g., law enforcement, courts) holding the abuser accountable for the abuse they inflict.

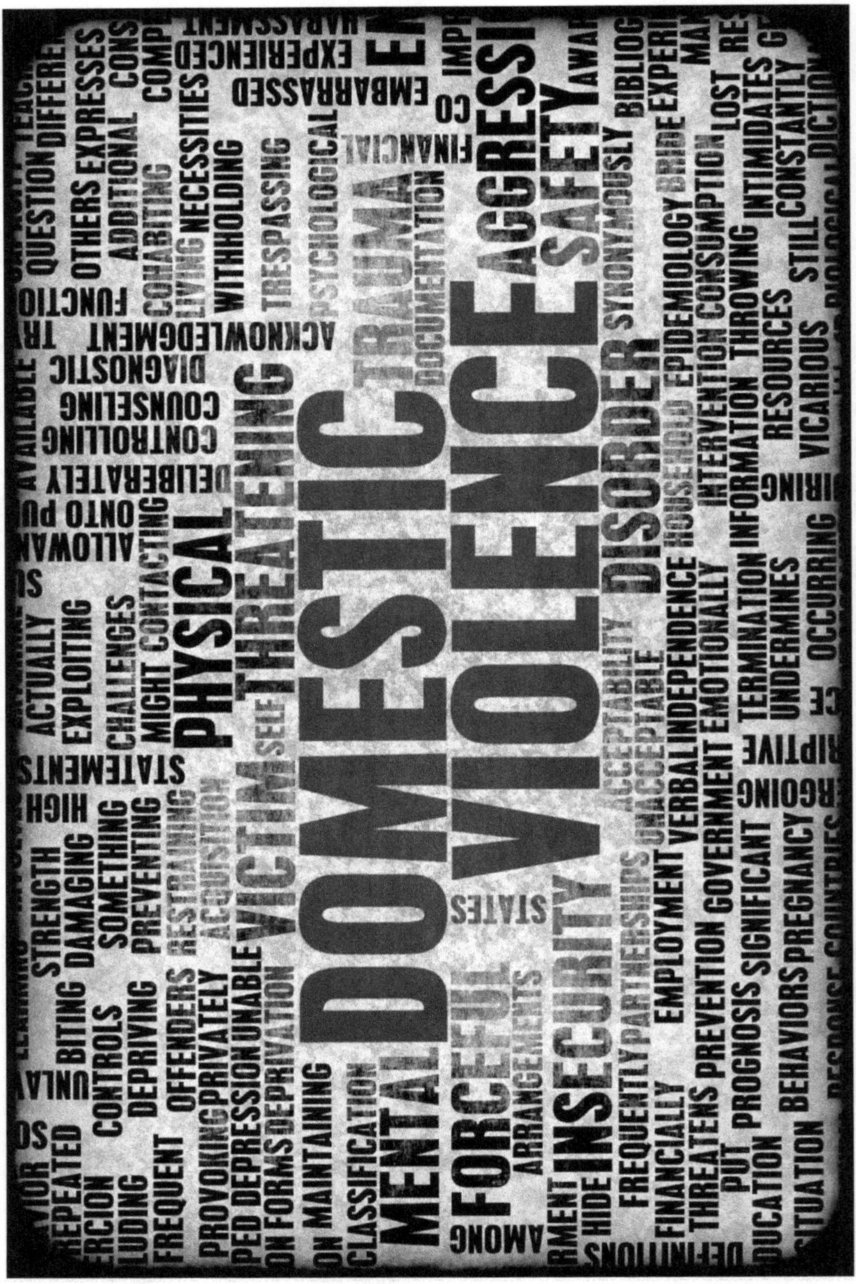
DOMESTIC
VIOLENCE
PHYSICAL
THREATENING
VICTIM
TRAUMA
AGGRESSI
SAFETY
DISORDER
INSECURITY
FORCEFUL
MENTAL

About The Author

Donna L. Quesinberry, known as "Q," is a literary alchemist—transforming silence into verse, and survival into empowered narrative. As solopreneur of dpInk Ltd. Liability Company, and President of DonnaInk Publications, she cultivates platforms that celebrate diverse voices and elevate transformative storytelling.

With more than 20,000 authored works spanning 100+ disciplines for global clients, Quesinberry blends creative innovation with strategic precision. Her poetry reveals the unspoken truths of feminine resilience and spiritual reckoning, becoming both balm and battle cry.

In *Stolen Lullabies & Secret Impasses*, she invites readers into a lyrical sanctuary of healing, launching *the Voices Beyond the Impasse: The Reclamation Movement* to amplify survivor stories and rewrite the silence. A devoted mother, grandmother, and faith-filled leader, Q resides in metropolitan Washington, DC, where her words continue to bridge art, advocacy, and awakening.

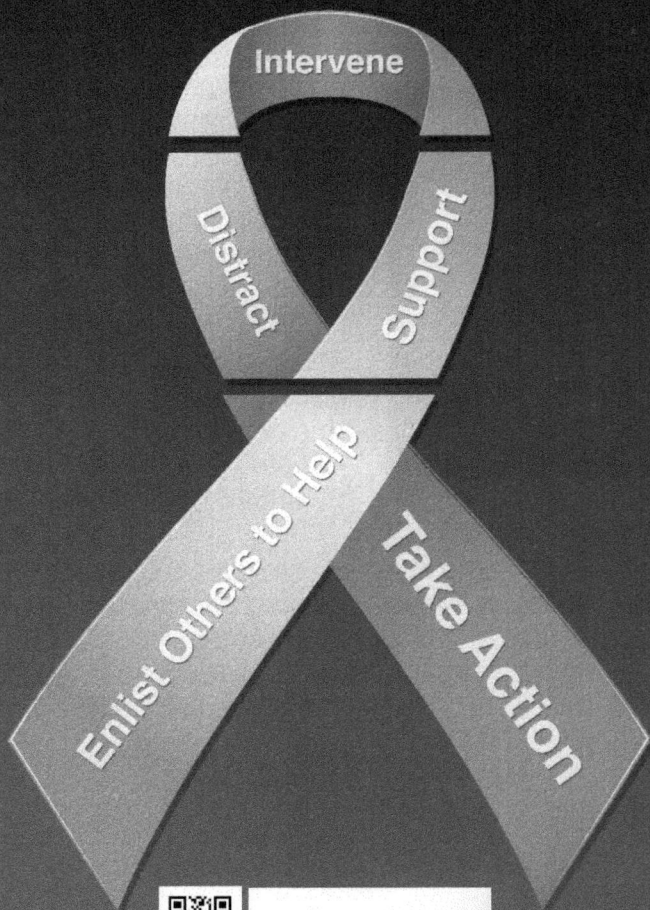

Visit the Author

Donna L. Quesinberry is available for events, radio and television speaking and presentations. And her professional services remain a viable part of her day-to-day life as an expert in empowerment, business intelligence and strategy, proposal direction and training of all the above.

Facebook:
https://www.facebook.com/donnalquesinberry
https://www.facebook.com/donnainkpublications
https://www.facebook.com/msdonnalquesinberry

LinkedIn:
https://www.linkedin.com/in/donnaink

Pinterest:
https://www.pinterest.com/donnaink

Tik Tok
@msdonnalquesinberry | @donnainkpublications

Twitter:
https://twitter.com/donnaink

Website:
http://www.donnalquesinberry.com
http://www.donnaink.shop

IT'S TIME … TO TALK ABOUT IT!

Your voice. Our future. Prevent sexual violence.

About Sage Sweetwater

Sage Sweetwater provided the Foreword for *Stolen Lullabies & Secret Impasses* and her love for pulp fiction dime store novels has re-invented the way audience thinks. She goes beyond the conventional and breaks through the door to a more imaginative property. She converts obstacles into opportunities, innovative and operating within her audience's understanding. She knows what strengths she can count on when under fire. Sage Sweetwater is a pathfinder, blessed with being born gifted and with natural insulation, registering in the upper bracket of talent and well-being, doing something worthwhile in culture, focusing on inner achievements as well as her outer attainments. Her process of writing is finding alternative paths through the maze of life.

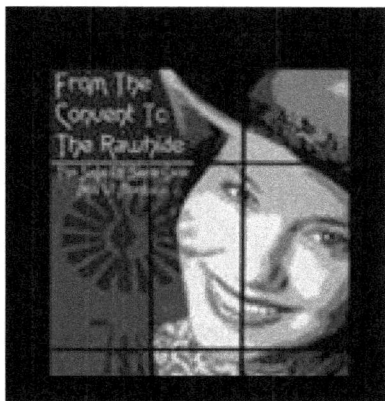

Sage Sweetwater hopes her own name will surface as one of a notable woman in history. Women outlaws are nothing new. We exist in every century, traveling with copyright as our companion. Books are a viable "stagecoach" in which Sage Sweetwater may travel with sizzling page turners in her satchel that Calamity Jane and Wild Bill Hickok may have taken out in trade for pistols and whiskey. Sage Sweetwater says it's a fair trade, a story for a Colt and firewater.

AWARENESS +

Action

=social change

Domestic Violence
Awareness Month

Visit Sage Sweetwater

AuthorsDen
http://www.authorsden.com/sagesweetwater

LinkedIn
http://www.linkedin.com/in/sagesweetwater

Other Donna L. Quesinberry Works

Books (Nonfiction, Fiction, & Evergreen)

50 Million Things Since Sunday Day Planner & Journal

A Boy and His Dog: Best Life Book of Self-Discovery Journal

A Casual Guy's Journal

A Time for Faith (Soul Symphony series)

An Introduction To Enterprise Architecture – Chapter Q&A, Case Studies, Essays

Awakening Wisdom (Soul Symphony series)

Book Development 101

Creative Cursive Handwriting Exercise Book: "I Can Write" for K ds

Diva In the Making Journal

Eisenhower And Civil Rights – Editor and Desktop Publisher

Elevated Details (Soul Symphony series)

Equine Lover's Journal

Faces of Rap Mothers Fathers' Editions series (Books One through Ten)

Faces of Rap Mothers Presents . . . varied Artisans series (Books One through Ten)

Faces of Rap Mothers series (Books One through Ten)

Faces of Rap Mothers: Rap Mothers Save The Day series (Children's One through Ten)

Fashion Squatch

Fashion Squatch Day Planner

From Thrift to Thriving: A Thrift Collector's Organizing Journal

Heavenly Sent Messages

Holding Fast: Daily Remembrances

I, Myself, Am Strange and Unusual
Illuminating Shadows: A Journey from a Higher Realm of Existence
Kittycat Journal
Laughter and Other Considerations
My Guardian ~ My Angel (Soul Symphony series)
Naturally Endowed: Chaos by Decree
No Beauty Shines Brighter Than A Good Heart Journal
Nurses Rock Journal
Over 100 Mandalas for Colorists Living Life
Sacred Notations Poetry Prompt Journal
Sea Nymphs Journal
See Clearly in the Present
Skate Notes
Skate Notes II: Revenge of the Skate Notes
Special Angels: Yes! You Have Special Angels
Spy Girl Journal
Spy Guy Journal
Squatch Thoughts: Take It From A Squatch
Stolen Lullabies & Secret Impasses, Editions 1 and 2
Stolen Lullabies & Vanished Grace, Volume 2
Loving the Whole Self: Through a Shadow Work Prompt Journal
The Little Things (Halloween Helping Guide)
The Vale Protocol
Ultimate Faces of Rap Mothers Guidebook
Vino Lover's Journal & Planner
Winter's Notes: A Seasonal Journal
Women Who Gain Credibility (Soul Symphony series)
Your Soul ~ Your Magic (Soul Symphony series)

Magazines & Publications

DonnaInk Publications
Katsujinken, A Sword Arts Journal – Publisher and Contributor

Washington Gas

Journalism ♀ Syndicated Columns

"Some Girls" Helps Teens Avoid The Pitfalls Of Youth

"Whistleblower Protection Enhancement Act Of 2010" Passes Senate

1 - 2 April 2011 – Blue Ridge Writers' Conference

100 Years Of American Poetry – 1910-2010

10-13 April, Federal Senior Management Conference

2010 Acs National Student Writing Competition

2010 Diversity Council Honors

2011 Writer Schedule!

2013 Grandmaster, Writer Advocate, And Equestrian, Ann C. Crispin dies at age 63

20th Symposium for Professional Food Writers

25 March 2011 – Minority Business Expo

27 - 29 June 2011 – Cyber Warfare 6 Security Summit

40 Yr. Rock 'N' Roll Engineering Veteran Releases His Access All Areas Memoir

4th Annual Improvised Explosive Day Of Golf: Chevy Chase Club, June 2011

5th Annual Intelligence And Processing Summit, 16-18 November 2009

8th Annual Light Armored Vehicles & Stryker Summit In

8th Image Fusion Conference, 16 November 2009

9/11/2011 Marks The 10th Anniversary Of 9/11/2001

A Best-Seller On Amazon, But Not A Lot Of Sales?

A Cry For Uniformity In American Public Education

A Fourth Estate Christmas Story

A Military Future With E-Camouflage And The Cloak Of Invisibility

A National Writing Examiner (NWE) Reminder!

A Soldier's Thoughts About Iraq And Afghanistan

A Strong Middle Class (Task Force And Executive Orders)

A Volunteer Information Starter-Kit For The Deepwater Horizon Response

Achieving Optimal Healthcare For The Warfighter Via Inter-Agency Collaboration

Achieving Timely, Accurate, And Relevant Intelligence

Acquisition Workforce Development Strategic Plan For 2010-2014

Act Of Toleration

AFCEA Symposium Sets The Barometer Regarding Emerging Technologies

Affordable Care Act: The Showdown At O' We May Congressional Closeout

Aiding Government End Clients In Social Media Growth

Ai-Kon (Animation) Convention Information

Air Force One The Final Mission: Interview With Co-Authors Joel, Michael Cohen

Always By Their Side - An Urgent Message For Wounded Heroes From The USO

Amazon Heads To Russia

Amvets Supports The Washington Dc Wounded
Angels

Announcing, Mountains Of The Sea By Günter O. Swoboda

Anticipating Plan X, DARPA'S Cyberwarfare Solution

April is Poetry Month

Are We Missing Something

Are you influenced?

Are you ready for the Annual Self-Published Book Awards?

ARRA (American Recovery and Reinvestment Act) for information technology (IT)

ASJA Annual Writer's Conference

Author of "The Pharm House," Bill Powers Talks About ITW's ThrillerFest IX

Author Sean Adkins's New Title 'Wolfen: Bloodlines' Is A Horror Lover's Treat

Backspace Agent-Author Seminar In New York City

Barack Obama's Wild Ride

Barefoot Book's Adherence To Grassroots Initiatives

Barnes And Noble Nook Press Replaces Pubit

Bestselling Titles January Through March 2013

Brainstorming, What Is Your Inner Source?

Bridges

Bring Your Own Device And Information Safety

Build Your Business Identity

Business Events For June In And Around Washington DC

Business Intelligence And You - Driving New BI Trends

Characters What, Who, Why?

Cigarettes: The Golden Albatross

Claus As A Candidate

Clean Contracting Act And Continued Middle-Firm Abuse

Closure Of The Business Transformation Agency (BTA)

Cockrell Engineering Students Design And Separate Two Satellites In Space

Competitive Bidding And The New Administration's Fiscal Agenca

Congressional Impetus Toward Fahrenheit

Copyright Infringement And Misrepresentation

Copyright To Be Or Not To Be?

Cost-Effective Contracting Without Gouging?

Crack Me Once Shame On You-Part 1

Crack Me Twice Shame On Me-Part 2

Cracker Beware, How To Arbitrate WIPO Infractions

Cryptic Language And The Art Of Communication

Cultural Consciousness And The Media

Cyber Security And The Fourth Estate

DARPA Introduces Transformer (The Flying HMMWV)

Deadlines And The Freelance Writer

Debut Medical Mystery Thriller Novel, The Pharm House By Bill Powers

Debut, Indie, Self-Published Or Vanity And Publishing

Delivering A Quality Business Email

Deltek's INPUT Contract Predictions For 2011

Demarchy, Fifth In The Ten-Part Series On Global Constructs

Department Of Defense (DOD) Business Transformation Agency (BTA) EP&I Title 5 Violations (Part 1)

Department Of Defense (DOD) Business Transformation Agency (BTA) EP&I Title 5 Violations (Part 2)

Department Of Defense (DOD) Inspector General Hotline

Department Of Defense Releases Updated Wounded Warrior Handbook

Department Of Defense's (DOD's) Innovation For New Value, Efficiency & Savings Tomorrow (INVEST)

Department Of Justice Settles With Three Of The Major Publishing Houses

Diamonds Are Forever

Discovery Fly Over Delivers Majestic Panoply For Washingtonians

DMA (Defense Media Activity) Moved To Ft. Meade

Freedom Of The Press Forever

From My Friend David Axelrod And The White House

From TBI Survivor To Future Best-Selling Author, Saverio Monachino Delivers

FUTURE | Sharing The World Sisterhood III - Leadership Conference 2009

GAO Makes 11 Recommendations To DOD To Improve Fellowships And Training Programs

GBE101: Adding Slide Shares To The Business Development Arsenal

GBE101: Economic Woes And The Consignment Promises Of Tomorrow

GBE101: Government Contracting

GBE101: Government Proposal Improvement Processes

GBE101: Grant (Sponsored Project) Funding, Part 1 Of 14

GBE101: Incorporating Optogenetics Into Your Business Scheme

GBE101: Navigating Change In A Perpetually Evolving Virtual Environment

GBE101: Podcasting - Becoming A Technological Native

GBE101: Social Network Sites (SNS)

GBE101: Strategies For Business Development Under The Social Network Umbrella

GBE101: The Downside Of Social Network Service (SNS) Websites, Part 1

GBE101: The Downside Of Social Network Service (SNS) Websites, Part 2

GBE101: The Downside Of Social Network Service (SNS) Websites, Part 3

GBE101: Vodcasting Or Videographies

GBE101: Webinars

GBE101: Wikis And Wikipedia

GBE's City Secret: Free National Park Week In Washington DC

Global Constructs

Global Democratization, Eighth In A Ten-Part Series On Global Constructs

Google+ (Google Plus) Or - ?

Government Business 101: United States Constitution, The Executive Branch And Federal Contracting

Government Business And The New Marching Orders, Part 1

Government Business And The New Marching Orders, Part 2

Government Business Examiner (GBE) Event List For September 2010

Government Business Examiner (GBE) Introduces Washington Network Group (WNG)

Government Business Examiner News Columnist

Government Contract Administrators Identify With FBO.Gov

Memes

Memetic Journalism, Part One

Memetic Journalism, Part Two

Microsoft Office 365 Beta Is Available – Sign Up Today

Military Technology News Columnist
Military Technology News Columnist

MITRE Announces Open Competition Encouraging Federal Government Tech Innovation

Mobile App For Wounded Warriors

Modern Warfighter Full Motion Video And UAS Surveillance

Monthly Editorial Submission

Mormon And The Moundbuilders

Multi-Level Integrated Command, Control And Communications Air Defense (MIC4AD)

Multi-Sensor And Intelligence Fusion

'Narrative Magazine' Story Contest

Narrative Magazine's Fall 2009 Story Contest

Narrative, Bringing Great Literature To The World Online

National "Get Caught Reading Month" Is May!
National Harbor, Festival Of Lights

National Novel Writing Month (NaNoWriMo) Municipal Liaisons Wanted For 2010

National Novel Writing Month Is Only Fifteen Days Away

National Poetry Month – Join In The Celebration!

National Writing Examiner (NWE) 101: Constructive Or Destructive Criticism

National Writing Examiner (NWE) 101: The Consultant Proposal

National Writing Examiner (NWE) 101: The Federal Acquisition Proposal

National Writing Examiner (NWE) 101: The Grant Proposal

National Writing Examiner (NWE) Presents Poetry Readings For National Poetry Month

National Writing Examiner Interviews Emerging Young Adult Author Jeannie Palmer

National Writing Examiner Interviews Michael Rushnak, Best-Selling Author

National Writing Examiner Introduces Mr. Bryan Thomas's, Make A Life Training Series

National Writing Examiner News Columnist

NATO At Fifty – Editor
Necessary" Premium Pricing

Neuro-Literature Research

New Age Perspectives Columnist

New Age Perspectives News Columnist
New Age Perspectives News Columnist

New Female Protective Gear Prototype

No Affordable Housing

Non-Encrypted Identification Theft

Northern Virginia Based Contractors Face 25 - 40 Years In Prison

Nuclear Security Summit - Washington DC

NWE 101: How To Skype Writer Interviews With Scripting And A Storyboard

NWE 101: Writing And Data Storage Devices

NWE Info 101: The World Wide Web (WWW) And The Content Writer

NWE Introduces Katherine Kane's, Training The City Dog & City Dog Books

NWE Introduces Our Knoxville Recreation Examiner Rick Brown's Book "Ranger Up!"

NWE-101: An Overview Of Publishing Markets For The New Or Emergent Author

NWE101: Author Basics

NWE101: Business Writing And Customer Relationship Management

NWE101: Dispelling The Myths Of Proposal Writing

NWE101: For The Ghost In You

NWE101: Genre Basics

NWE101: How Does A Grant Writer Get The "Best Score?"

NWE101: Is A Manuscript Evaluation A Good Idea

NWE101: Statistics, Graphics And Presentation Of The Grant Writer

NWE101: The Art Of Grant Writing, Part 1

NWE101: The Book Proposal

NWE101: The Business Proposal

NWE101: The Humanities

NWE101: The Marriage Proposal

NWE101: Typesetting, Templates, Design Layouts And The Business Writer's Rights

NWE101: Where Are The Grammar Police?

NWE101: Writing Industry

OED (Oxford English Dictionary) Adds New Words

Officer (A Washington DC Resident)

Panhandler Paradise

Pass Along National Pay Hikes

Pentagon's Cyberspace Strategy Is Good News For Washington DC Businesses

Power, Protection, And Payload For The Family Of Light Armored Vehicles (FOLAV)

Practical Virtualization Solutions: Virtualization From The Trenches

Pre-Engineering Your Job Search In Washington DC

President Barack Obama Announces The Chief Technology
President Barack Obama Declares H1N1 Emergency

President Barack Obama Signs Executive Order To Improve Access To Mental Health

President Obama And The New Transparency

President Obama Unveils The 2013 Budget At Nova - Annandale Virginia

President Obama's Decision On Afghanistan Today - 1 December 2009 –
President Obama's Homeowner Affordability And Stability Plan

Press Release: Colorado Author's Reviews For "Kid's Flicks (Dad's Picks)
Press Release: FTC Publishes Final Guides Governing Endorsements, Testimonials

Press Release: President Obama And Modernizing Intelligence: Statement Of Support
By Third Way

Pricing A New Book Title

Procurement Institute Of Americas Will Be Resource For International Procurement
Community

Provisions Of The Act-American Recovery And Reinvestment Act Of 2009

Putting Spirit Into The Business Marriage

Radio Frequency Identification (RFID)

Radio Interviews, The Author's Role

Ragged Right Or Justified, What Is The Right Way To Lay A Book Out?

Readability Standards, IQ, And The Fourth Estate Part One

Readability Standards, IQ, And The Fourth Estate Part Two

Real Warriors Campaign

Recovery.Gov & President Obama's Stimulus Plan

Recreational Resources Needed

Red Badge Of Courage, Introduction

Registration For Public Procurement Conference Of The Americas

Reinventing The Workforce - The Virtual Workforce (VW) Community

Release Of Living The Dream By Mr. Tim Baker

Release Of The Maternity Labyrinth, By Ariel Balter

The Politics Of Governmentese And The Illusion Of Change Management

The Public Procurement Of The Americas Conference In Washington DC

The State Of The Fourth Estate

The Tao Te Ching And The Trayvon Martin Case

The Top Social Media Sites For 2014

The U.S. Government Channel Launches On YouTube

The United States Government Channel On YouTube

Theories On The Physical Basis Of PSI (i.e.: ESP and PK

Thermal Vacuum Testing Of Navy's MUOS (Mobile User Objective System) Completed

They've Shutdown, But Why Isn't Anyone Protesting?

Those Collectible Recipes

Time Management Through Submission Analysis

Tinged Bassinet With Verbs, Performance Poetry-Blackmail Press

To Agree Or Disagree - Is That The Question In Social Media Threads?

Total VMT May Force InVirtual And Telework Participant Increases

Turbotap.Org Connects US Military To Money, Benefits And Jobs

Understanding Your Message

United States Army's Warrior Transition Command

United World Awakening, Sixth In A Ten-Part Series On Global Constructs

Universalizing RFP (Proposal) Writing Tips, Part One

University Course

Up To My Ears In America, Memoir Of Escape From Communist Czechoslovakia

Upcoming Writer Contests

US Navy Cyber Command Now Located At Ft. Meade

USAF X51-A And U.S. Army AHW Both Tested Successfully

USO Wounded Warrior Centers Restore Health & Wellness During Walter Reed BRAC

Vassar Miller Prize In Poetry For 2012 Due 15 November 2011

Viral Impressions Of Gifted Minds

Virginia Kenshinkai's 2011 Swordfest - 13-15 May 2011

Virtual Combat IED Simulation At Camp Atterbury Joint Maneuver Training Center

Vision

Vote With Heart And Hand

Vote Your Conscience

Writer 101: Developing The Inner Source

Writer 101: Social Network Sites (SNS) And Personal Information Archives

Writer Conferences For 2010 And Beyond, Part 1

Writer Conferences For 2010 And Beyond, Part 2

Writer Resource List: Online Writing Communities

Writer's Digest Science Fiction | Fantasy Competition

Writer's Digest Editors' Intensive September 11-12, 2010

Writer's Digest: Popular Fiction Awards 2010

Writer's Market: Available Courses For April 2010

Writers Write

Writing 101: Developing The Holistic Writer

Writing 101: How To Craft Your Book Of Remembrance

Writing 101: Personal Definition As A Writer - Part 1

Writing 101: Personal Definition As A Writer - Part 2

Writing 101: Rating Personal Literary Performance

Writing 101: Resources For Establishing Your Writing Goals - Part 1

Writing 101: Resources For Establishing Your Writing Goals - Part 2

Writing 101: Resources For Establishing Your Writing Goals - Part 3

Writing 101: Strengthening Writer Qi

Writing 101: Stress And Writer's Block - Part One

Writing 101: Stress And Writer's Block - Part Two

Writing 101: Techniques, Imagery, And Beginning Exercises - Part 1

Writing 101: Techniques, Imagery, And Beginning Exercises - Part 2

Writing 101: Techniques, Imagery, And Beginning Exercises - Part 3

Writing 101: Techniques, Imagery, And Beginning Exercises - Part 4

Writing 101: Techniques, Imagery, And Beginning Exercises - Part 5

Writing 101: Techniques, Imagery, And Beginning Exercises - Part 6

Writing 101: Techniques, Imagery, And Beginning Exercises - Part 7

Writing 101: Uniting With The Inner Voice - Part One

Writing 101: Uniting With The Inner Voice - Part Two

Writing 101: Whatever The Mind Of Man Can Conceive And Believe, It Can Achieve

Writing A Declarative Statement Or Essay - Using The Declaration Of Independence

Writing And The Tree Of Life

Join The Mailing List!

In order to become aware of events, interviews, signings, speaking engagements and presentations remit an email to: slasi@donnaink.com and put "Mailing List" in the subject line. Special discounts will become available for mailing list members . . . so be certain to send an email confirming your interest!

The *Voices Beyond the Impasse: The Reclamation Movement* invites readers to email: donnaink@gmail.com for more information on how to participate.

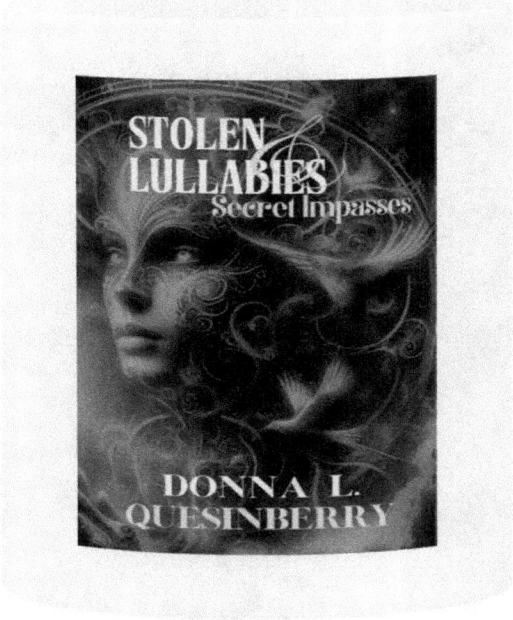

Resources

Child Abuse and Neglect Awareness Resources

Federal Interagency Work Group on Child Abuse and Neglect
Please visit these agencies to see how their programs support child abuse prevention in your community. More information about the Work Group and its members, including contact information, can be found on the Children's Bureau at:

http://www.acf.hhs.gov/programs/cb/fediawg

U.S. Department of Health and Human Services (HHS)
Office on Child Abuse and Neglect, Children's Bureau, Administration on Children, Youth and Families (ACYF)

Administration for Children and Families (ACF)

Child Welfare Information Gateway, ACYF, ACF

Family Violence Prevention and Services Program, Family and Youth Services Bureau (FYSB), ACYF, ACF

Child Care Bureau, Office of Family Assistance, ACF

Division of Child and Family Development, Office of Planning, Research and Evaluation (OPRE), ACF

Office of Refugee Resettlement, ACF

Office of Human Services Policy, Office of the Assistant Secretary for Planning and Evaluation (ASPE)

Division of Behavioral Health, Indian Health Service (IHS)

Office of Minority Health

Office of Behavioral and Social Sciences Research, National Institutes of Health (NIH)

Child Development and Behavior Branch, National Institute of Child Health and Human Development, NIH

Child Abuse and Neglect Program, Division of Developmental Translational Research, National Institute of Mental Health, NIH

Center for Substance Abuse Treatment (CSAT), Office of Policy, Coordination and Planning, Substance Abuse and Mental Health Services Administration (SAMHSA)

Maternal and Child Health Bureau, Division of Healthy Start and Perinatal Services, Health Resources and Services Administration

Division of Violence Prevention, National Center for Injury, Prevention and Control, Centers for Disease Control and Prevention (CDC)

U.S. Department of Agriculture
National Institute of Food and Agriculture (NIFA)

U.S. Department of Defense
Family Advocacy Program, Military Community and Family Policy, Office of the Deputy Under Secretary of Defense

U.S. Department of Education
Office of Special Education and Rehabilitative Services, Office of Special Education Programs

U.S. Department of the Interior
Bureau of Indian Affairs

U.S. Department of Justice
Victim and Victimization Research Division, Office of Research and Evaluation, National Institute of Justice (NIJ), Office of Justice Programs (OJP)

Office for Victims of Crime, OJP

Office on Violence Against Women

OJP Office of Juvenile Justice and Delinquency Prevention (OJJDP)

Child Protection Division, OJJDP, OJP

U.S. Department of State
Office to Monitor and Combat Trafficking in Persons, Under Secretary for Democracy and Global Affairs

Commission to Eliminate Child Abuse and Neglect Fatalities

Sexual Assault Awareness Resources

The National Sexual Violence Resource Center (NSVRC) opened in July 2000 as a national information and resource hub relating to all aspects of sexual violence. Founded by the Pennsylvania Coalition Against Rape, the oldest and one of the largest state sexual assault coalitions, the NSVRC is funded through a cooperative agreement from the Centers for Disease Control and Prevention's Division of Violence Prevention.

The NSVRC staff collects and disseminates a wide range of resources on sexual violence including statistics, research, position statements, statutes, training curricula, prevention initiatives and program information. With these resources, the NSVRC assists coalitions, advocates and others interested in understanding and eliminating sexual violence. The NSVRC has an active and diverse Advisory Council that assists and advises staff and ensures a broad national perspective. The NSVRC also enjoys a strong partnership with state, territory and tribal anti-sexual assault coalitions and allied organizations.

In addition to tracking resources developed throughout the country, the NSVRC publishes a newsletter, The Resource, issues press releases and talking points on current events and coordinates an annual national sexual assault awareness month (SAAM) campaign in April.[14]

Child Sexual Abuse Prevention

Engaging Bystanders in Sexual Violence Prevention - this project highlights resources, research and tools that support the development of bystander intervention approaches to prevention.

http://www.nsvrc.org/projects/engaging-bystanders-sexual-violence-prevention

---

[14] This is an excerpt from the National Sexual Violence Resource Center (NSVRC) – the links are to their information – rather than hotlinks to victim resources – this is higher-end for developing campaigns and awareness initiatives. The author suggests researching for local resources for victims to have a well-formed arsenal of assistance in your awareness.

Health and Sexual Violence

Know Your Rights - *this section includes information for survivors of sexual violence and the general public about their rights.*

http://www.nsvrc.org/projects/know-your-rights-0

Lifespan

Multilingual Access - *this project is focused on fostering conversations that expand prevention and intervention across languages and cultures.*

http://www.nsvrc.org/projects/multilingual-access

National Sexual Assault Conference

National Sexual Assault Conference

http://www.nsvrc.org/projects/national-sexual-assault-conference

Preventing Sexual Violence in Disasters

Preventing Sexual Violence in Disasters

http://www.nsvrc.org/projects/preventing-sexual-violence-disasters

Rape Prevention and Education

Rape Prevention and Education (RPE)

http://www.nsvrc.org/projects/rape-prevention-and-education-rape

Rural

SANE Sustainability - *this collaborative project with the International Association of Forensic Nurses and Office on Violence Against Women, provides free training, technical assistance, and consultation to local SANE programs and State/Territory and Tribal SANE Coordinators.*

http://www.nsvrc.org/projects/sane-sustainability

Sexual Abuse in Detention Resource Center - *the National Sexual Violence in Detention Education and Resource Project (NSDVERP) provides technical assistance to rape crisis centers, state sexual assault coalitions, and correctional facilities to address the challenges of implementing sexual assault response teams in correctional environments.*

http://www.nsvrc.org/projects/NSDVERP

Sexual Assault Demonstration Initiative

Sexual Assault Demonstration Initiative

http://www.nsvrc.org/projects/sexual-assault-demonstration-initiative

Sexual Assault Response Teams

Sexual Assault Response Teams

http://www.nsvrc.org/projects/sexual-assault-response-teams-sart-0

EVERY 15 SECONDS, A WOMAN IS BATTERED IN THE US. — US dept of Justice

CALL NATIONAL DOMESTIC HOTLINE
1.800.799.SAFE
1.800.799.7233

STOP DOMESTIC VIOLENCE.

Domestic Violence Awareness Resources

National Coalition of Domestic Violence Awareness

The National Coalition Against Domestic Violence (NCADV), has worked since 1978 to make every home a safe home. NCADV works to raise awareness about domestic violence; to educate and create programming and technical assistance, to assist the public in addressing the issue, and to support those impacted by domestic violence.[15]

The National Domestic Violence Hotline

1-800-799-7233 (SAFE)

www.ndvh.org

Domesticshelters.org

Free, online, searchable database of domestic violence shelter programs nationally –

www.domesticshelters.org

National Dating Abuse Helpline

1-866-331-9474

www.loveisrespect.org

---

[15]   This section is taken from the National Coalition of Domestic Violence Awareness website – for victim services contact 911 and/or local resources. It is good to become aware of the resources in your area to combat domestic violence while working on an awareness campaign.

Americans Overseas Domestic Violence Crisis Center International Toll-Free (24/7)

1-866-USWOMEN (879-6636)

www.866uswomen.org

National Child Abuse Hotline/Child help

1-800-422-4453

www.childhelp.org

National Sexual Assault Hotline

1-800-656-4673 (HOPE)

www.rainn.org

National Suicide Prevention Lifeline

1-800-273-8255

www.suicidepreventionlifeline.org

National Center for Victims of Crime

1-202-467-8700

www.victimsofcrime.org

National Human Trafficking Resource Center/Polaris Project

Call: 1-888-373-7888 | Text: HELP to BeFree (233733)

www.polarisproject.org

National Network for Immigrant and Refugee Rights

1-510-465-1984

www.nnirr.org

National Coalition for the Homeless

1-202-737-6444

www.nationalhomeless.org

Children

Childhelp USA/National Child Abuse Hotline

1-800-422-4453

www.childhelpusa.org

Children's Defense Fund

202-628-8787

www.childrensdefense.org

Child Welfare League of America

202-638-2952

www.cwla.org

National Council on Juvenile and Family Court Judges

Child Protection and Custody/Resource Center on Domestic Violence -
1-800-527-3233 –

www.ncjfcj.org

Center for Judicial Excellence

info@centerforjudicialexcellence.org
www.centerforjudicialexcellence.org

Teens

Love is Respect

Hotline: 1-866-331-9474

www.loveisrespect.org

Break the Cycle

202-824-0707

www.breakthecycle.org

Differently Abled

Domestic Violence Initiative

(303) 839-5510 / (877) 839-5510

www.dviforwomen.org

Deaf Abused Women's Network (DAWN)

Email: Hotline@deafdawn.org | VP: 202-559-5366 –

www.deafdawn.org

Women of Color

Women of Color Network

1-800-537-2238

www.wocninc.org

INCITE! Women of Color Against Violence

incite.natl@gmail.com

www.incite-national.org

Latina/Latino

Alianza

1-505-753-3334

www.dvalianza.org

Casa de Esperanza

Linea de crisis 24-horas/24-hour crisis line 1-651-772-1611

www.casadeesperanza.org

Indigenous Women

National Indigenous Women's Resource Center

855-649-7299

www.niwrc.org

Indigenous Women's Network

1-512-258-3880

www.indigenouswomen.org

Asian/Pacific Islander

Asian and Pacific Islander Institute on Domestic Violence

1-415-954-9988

www.apiidv.org

Committee Against Anti-Asian Violence (CAAAV)

1-212- 473-6485

www.caaav.org

Manavi

1-732-435-1414

www.manavi.org

African-American

Institute on Domestic Violence in the African American Community

1-877-643-8222

www.dvinstitute.org

The Black Church and Domestic Violence Institute

1-770-909-0715

www.bcdvi.org

Lesbian, Bi-Sexual, Gay, Transgender, Gender Non-Conforming

The Audre Lorde Project

1-178-596-0342

www.alp.org

LAMBDA GLBT Community Services

1-206-350-4283

http://www.qrd.org/qrd/www/orgs/avproject/main.htm

National Coalition of Anti-Violence Programs

1-212-714-1184

www.ncavp.org

National Gay and Lesbian Task Force

1-202-393-5177

www.ngltf.org

Abuse in Later Life

National Clearinghouse on Abuse in Later Life

1-608-255-0539

www.ncall.us

National Center for Elder Abuse

1-855-500-3537

http://www.ncea.aoa.gov/

Men

National Organization for Men Against Sexism (NOMAS)

1-720-466-3882

www.nomas.org

A Call to Men

1-917-922-6738

www.acalltomen.org

Men Can Stop Rape

1-202-265-6530

www.mencanstoprape.org

Men Stopping Violence

1-866-717-9317

www.menstoppingviolence.org

Legal

American Bar Association Commission on Domestic Violence

1-202-662-1000

www.abanet.org/domviol

Battered Women's Justice Project

1-800-903-0111

www.bwjp.org

Legal Momentum

1-212-925-6635

www.legalmomentum.org

Womenslaw.org

www.womenslaw.org

National Clearinghouse for the Defense of Battered Women

1-800-903-0111 x 3

www.ncdbw.org

October is Domestic Violence Awareness Month

Together we can end
domestic abuse

Moondust Media

dpInk

Donnalnk Publications, L.L.C.

Publisher
www.donnaink.shop

For bulk orders, special orders, etc.

Special Markets Division
DonnaInk Publications, L.L.C.
17611 Aquasco Road
Annapolis, MD 20613
Email: submissions@gmail.com

For Promotions:
Promotions Division
DonnaInk Publications, L.L.C.
17611 Aquasco Road
Annapolis, MD 20613
Email: donna.quesinberry@donnaink.shop

ZENCON ART OF
ZEN CONSULTANCY
PR & Marketing